CHANGING DIMENSIONS OF LIBRARY AND INFORMATION SCIENCE STUDIES

CHANGING DIMENSIONS OF LIBRARY AND INFORMATION SCIENCE STUDIES

CHANGING DIMENSIONS OF LIBRARY AND INFORMATION SCIENCE STUDIES

ABDUL BAQUEE
ISHFAQ AHMED PALLA

Ess Ess Publications
New Delhi

CHANGING DIMENSIONS OF LIBRARY AND INFORMATION SCIENCE STUDIES

ISBN : 978-93-87698-88-8

Price : 650/-

First Published 2021

Published by:
Ess Ess Publications
4831/24, Ansari Road,
Darya Ganj,
New Delhi-110 002.
INDIA
Phones: 23260807, 41563444
Fax: 41563334
E-mail: info@essessreference.com
www.essessreference.com

Cover Design by *Patch Creative Unit*

Printed and bound in India

Contents

Preface

1 Use of Mobile Technologies in Educational Settings In 21st Century 1

2 Application of Radio-frequency Identification (RFID) Technology in Library and Information Centers 14

3 Web 2.0 and Library 2.0 31

4 Digital Library 43

5 Information Literacy, Digital Information Literacy, Media and information Literacy in Indian Perspective 60

6 Go for Green (G4G) : A Sustainable Development Approach in and of Library and Information Centres 83

7 Library in the Horizon of Knowledge Management and Knowledge Harvesting 99

Preface

With the emergence of Information Technology, significant developments have taken place all across globe. Keeping these rapid developments in mind, the functions of the social, economic and academic institutions from the different corners of the globe had undergone a big change. In the cotemporary world, almost every institution/ organization makes heavily use of novel information technologies. Libraries over the years have been at the forefront of adopting the modern technologies to carry out their functions. From Cataloguing Cards to Floppy Discs to CD-ROMS to OPACs to Web Discovery services, the libraries are not lagging behind in implementing the novel tools in carrying its day to day functions. Information stored in the libraries have taken major shifts from print to digital media. The technologies like RFID and QR are providing information and communication technology-based library services to increase the possible ways of fast and user-friendly services. The application of novel tools and technologies, prospects and challenges, awareness and use of innovative services in the libraries will lead us to enter into a transformed society.

The book mainly takes into account the importance of Knowledge Management (KM) in libraries. In addition, the topics like Information Literacy and Green Libraries are discussed in detail. Digital Libraries and Web 2.0 also form the part of the book.

The book is primarily written for the BLIS and MLIS students and it will immensely help students belonging to other subjects as well. In the modern times, enthusiasts who want to become information professionals will get great help relating to the different aspects of library organization. We hope that this book will enhance the knowledge of LIS professionals and to use the acquired knowledge in the possible areas on libraries.

The book is organised into 3 parts namely; Technology and Library, Emerging Trends in LIS Studies and Management in Library and Information Science and contains 6 chapters. Chapter 1: Mobile Technology (MT) deals with basic concept of mobile technology, role of MT in education as well as role of MT in library and information centers. Chapter 2: RFID in Library gives a holistic idea about RFIDs and how it can be useful to libraries. The chapter also tries to give a futuristic trend of RFID in libraries in India. Chapter 3: takes into account the different aspects of Web 2.0 in relation to the library services. The chapter includes the importance and role of blogs, wikis and other social media sites with regard to the different functions of the libraries.

Chapter 4: comprises of Digital Libraries, Services Provided by Digital Libraries, Need and Challenges, role of staff, Role of digital libraries in Learning and provides an overview of different National digital Libraries from the globe.Chapter 5:Information Literacy and Library comprises of different types of literacy in particular, Digital Literacy and Media Literacy. Several models related to information literacy given by eminent scholars and institutions are also taken into consideration in this chapter. Nevertheless, it also tries to focus on how do libraries can play an important role in developing literacy competencies among the mass. Chapter 6: discusses about what is green library and standards associated with green buildings. Some renowned green libraries all over the world are discussed here in brief and also what libraries can do with respect in fulfilling the UNESCO sustainable development goals are also highlighted here. Chapter 7: Libraries in the Horizon of Knowledge Management gives a concise insight on knowledge, its types, management of knowledge in library and other organization with a detailed account of historical development. How knowledge management environment can be developed and necessity of KM in library are also given due consideration.

Finally, in spite of our best efforts, some errors may still be left and we would appreciate to hear from the readers.

— Author

1

USE OF MOBILE TECHNOLOGIES IN EDUCATIONAL SETTINGS IN 21ST CENTURY

INTRODUCTION

Twenty first century is the era where teaching and learning irrespective of disciplines/subjects is not confined to the traditional classroom settings. Technology has become an irresistible part of our life style in the present century where we live in. Technology has altered many things in our daily routine. Nonetheless, Information Seeking Behaviour (ISB) has also undergone an enormous change since the beginning of second half of last century and that has reasonably happened due to development of Information and Communication Technologies (ICTs). Further, if we do microscopic analysis of ISB trends, then it is clear to us that one of the latest addition into the scientific inventions in the domain of ICTs is the development of Mobile Devices-a 'superstorm', which is also known as Mobile Technology or hand-held device

(Mayisela, 2013)has helped to change Information Seeking Behaviour (ISB) pattern. Eventually, in broader sense, it has changed our way of daily life. Now information is more fragmented in different forms such as text, image, audio, video and so on; and we use Mobile Technologies (MT) day in and day out to obtain this fragmented information (Wang et al. 2018). According to (Buarki & Dar, 2019) by 2020 almost 80 percent of total adults will have a smartphone worldwide. On the other side Statista (2017) [as cited by Law, Chan, & Wang (2018)] showed that by 2020 smartphone users will be more than 2.8 billion worldwide, and this figure will hold closer to one-third of the total global population. The same study also mentioned that an average adult spends four hours daily with his/ her smartphones for Social Networking (SN) or communication purpose. The mounting demand for high mobility and connectedness is the main driven factor of using MT more and more (Buarki & Dar, 2019).

It is said that today's youth are swimming in the pond of Mobile Technologies which is filled with internet technology, where it is also said that thinking of modern youths are different to their ancestors. Even some have criticized their brain as "physically different" (Dar, 2019). However, such technologies changed the behaviour people receive, disseminate and interact with very fast increasing ocean of information and pave the way of instantaneous channel of communication. This superstorm technology is equally well versed in all aspects of our life to complete our daily life cycle very smoothly. People are driving this vehicle -'Mobile Technologies' mainly for being in touch with friends, web navigation, seeking information, for amusement and much more and MTs has amplified the range of achieving the needs across geographical region, sectors and institutions (Hamad et al., 2017).

Use of Mobile devices has brought a dawn of new era. We are applying these technologies everywhere in our society; educational, commercial, social work purpose irrespective of profit making or non-profit making organizations ubiquitously.

WHAT IS MOBILE TECHNOLOGY?

Mobile Technologies (MTs) are handheld technological system that includes hardware (devices), software (programming interface and application software) and communication (networking services) feature. For instance, MTs are mobile phones, smart phones, portable digital assistants and integrated wireless enterprise solutions (Hamad et al., 2017). Unhelkar (2009) defined MT's:

> *a computing device small enough to hold and operate in the hand, many of these devices can connect to the Internet and interconnect with other devices (via Wi-Fi, Bluetooth, cellular networks or near field communication [NFC]). In general, integrate cameras, digital media players, and the ability to place and receive telephone calls and Global Positioning System (GPS) capabilities.*

Mobile or any handheld portable wireless devices,when connected with internet connectivity and allows users synchronously or asynchronously to connect via calls (video, audio) sending messages, and run different programming applications at anytime from anywhere.

Mobile technologies are able to run operating system or applications that can access internet and allow various activities such as downloads, accessing email services, able to provide information regarding location, weather forecasting and also have the equivalent capabilities to minicomputers and laptops (Jharotia, 2015).

EVOLUTION OF MOBILE TECHNOLOGY

Mobile wireless industry has gone through manifold evolution and changes since 1970s but specially, since 1990s it experienced very remarkable growth. The evolution of MTs is well demarcated as different generations (G) for example 1G, 2G...5G etc. The beginning of the network technology started with 0G in 1970s. During that period it was called as pre cellular mobile telephony technology such as Radio Telephones that were available in some cars. The next to 0G is 0.5G which is cluster of technology had advance feature than the prior 0G. These were the Radio Telephone, were the part of *Public Switch Telephone Network*, and mounted in cars or trucks. In 1979, Nippon Telephone Telegraph operated first cellular phone in Japan using 1St Generation of 1G. The period 1990s witnessed the stage of 2G or 2ndgeneration in Finland. It was offering the services like text message, picture messages and MMS. 3G first came in 2001 as commercial trial network by *NTT DoCoMo* in Japan, using*Wideband Code Division Multiple Access* (*WCDMA)* technology. By the end of 2007, the numbers of 3G subscribers were 295 million worldwide. 4G is next generation network technology having faster speed than the earlier 3G. 4G helped academics and R&D lab members to solve their problems associated with slow speed 3G technology (Mir & Kumar, 2015). Although in many places the trial of 5G technology has been done since last couple of years but officially not launched yet worldwide. Maybe in in a few years, we will have the access of super speed 5G technology within our hand. The 5G will make many impossible things possible within very lesser time and will bring a major revolution in the move of internet technology. Fifth Generation network technology may assist scientist and R&D lab staff a lot in their research and experiments.

USE OF MOBILE TECHNOLOGIES IN LIBRARIES

MTs are gradually becoming an integral part of human life and we use this technology to get access of information anytime and anywhere from around the world. As a result, large numbers of libraries are incorporating

MT's in order to provide their services which results the development of mobile library (Huang et al., 2015). As Wang et al., (2018) points;

> *Mobile library is the delivery of library services through wireless access using mobile devices to allow such activities as mobile searching and mobile reading. The service modes of mobile library include short message service, wireless application protocol and application for mobile terminals. 606p.*

The earliest library services which became possible to serve on Mobile Technology were Mobile OPACs, Mobile databases and Mobile library instruction. But with time, possibility of MTs in library has increased since many researches have carried out on it. Now with the advancement of MTs, libraries embrace this technology to provide few more services such as integrated library system, website on mobile, mobile electronic books, audio-visual library on mobile, reference services on mobile through SMS, email or some other way (Mansouri & Soleymani Asl, 2019).

Since the smartphones are compatible with multiple programming interfaces or application softwares, libraries can use MTs for number of purposes, for instance; marketing of library (library can create users network and promote the library by updating several library news, upcoming library as well as university events with its help), it can create a very healthy customer relationship, library can offer Current Awareness Services (CAS) on it in better way and also can do Selective Dissemination of Information services(SDI) very eloquently as the number of smartphone users are gaining very high momentum continuously. In addition, libraries can also use 'My Library' that enable the users to check individual profile and records, can track Inter library Loan, can request items, read alerts, new arrivals of books and journals as well. Further, library can create audio visual and virtual library tour, library location, orientation of library on MTs in a pretty effective way (Roy, 2017). Presently, MTs can also be used in libraries to scan Quick Response (QR) Code or 2D Barcode to get the access of information of library. For example, library can embed QR code links to library book shelves, can include online library tour, orientation, library website, registration for events, to get particular location of book etc. (Ashford, 2010).

MOBILE TECHNOLOGIES IN EDUCATION

Education is the fundamental right of any living human being.The *Universal Declaration ofHuman Rights* affirms that "*education* is a *fundamental human right*" for everyone. Every sector in the modern times are largely driven by Information and Communication Technologies and education is no exception. In recent years, the development and use of mobile devices, wireless communication and network technologies have been tremendously increasing in every organization, institution and sector i.e. business, politics, and defense economics and so on. Education plays a fundamental role in the development and progress of nation's economy. The 20th century education is highly different from the current one. Education in the 21st century has become highly a competitive process. The use of ICT equipment's in the modern schools, colleges and universities says it all about the educational set up in the 21st century. From the very beginning of the school age, the kids are given the education on ICT. Given the heavily prevalence of technology, students in their early school days are highly advanced and aware about the technology. Undoubtedly, "*world is changing*" and so do we. In order to prepare the new and younger generations to adopt this technological change in their educational set up, educational and technical institutions also need to change the strategies and ways that suit the current digital environment. The use of available technology must be used to benefit the students in the long term. However, there are few skills that early school students will need in order to become successful in the current environment. These include ability to use technology, ability to collaborate, inventing critical thinking skills, tendency to conduct research to find solutions to the problems. Mobile technologies can provide a great potential, if effectively designed, and implemented as such they become highly relevant in the socio-cultural context of education, learning and training. Mobile technologies have the potency to address to the diverse learning stylesby making the desired educational contents readily available to anyone, anywhere and anytime in the different formats texts audios, videos and so on. "The integration of mobile devices in the educational system presents enormous opportunities stretching from improved efficiency to accessibility of education to communities living in remote areas. The last decade has seen emergence of a new economy called Knowledge Economy, a fusion of globalization and Information and Communication Technology (ICT). Educationally advanced countries such as South Korea, USA, Japan, Taiwan, Singapore, Malaysia, European Union and Australia are using mobile devices in the educational sectors. These countries have been found promoting Mobile Learning (M-Learning) as a matter of national policies. They have accommodated e-Learning and m-Learning in their traditional learning systems. However, most of the Middle East countries are still out of race and facing number of challenges in M-Learning adoption"(Khan, Al-Shihi, Al-Khanjari, & Sarrab, 2015). However, at times using the Technology in educational context may give rise to unintended consequences i.e. learners becoming dependent while waiting and expecting the technology to find solutions to all problems (Routet, Levonen, &Biardeau, 2001). Use of mobile phones by the higher education students can let them to have greater access to communicate with the peers, guides anytime from anywhere. Moreover, students can establish social contacts and remain interconnected with the personalities of their interest (peers and other expert personnel to their related fields) all across the globe as sharing learning experiences can give useful academic support and students no longer remain restricted within the four walls of their educational institutions. Also, the open access movement has gained a momentum in the past few years, the academic community in general; researchers and faculties in particular can use the mobile technology for the good cause to meet their information needs.

1.1. Use of Mobile Technologies in Schools

After mothers lap, school is the next learning institution for any human being. There is significant impact of primary and secondary education on the students overall academic and social behaviour. Primary education is usually the starting phase of obligatory education in many countries. Education is not only about reading and writing but to shape our thinking and utilizing the knowledge for the growth. It helps us in developing the imagination at how one looks at his/her life. During early years, it is by education that helps students to develop mentally, physically and become socially aware. As they grow in age, they become highly aware and responsible of their roles and are the weapons to build their nations. While they are young, they think of taking their nations to the highest ranks. In schools we learn about facts and develop our basic skills. The contemporary education is highly different from that we used to get few decades before. In the developing and under developed countries, one can hardly think of using computers at the primary or secondary levels. *"The evolution of media from traditional to newer forms of digital media in the past decade has resulted in changes in the patterns of media use. For example, in 1970, children began to regularly watch TV at 4 years of age, whereas today, children begin interacting with digital media at 4 months of age"* (Chassiakos, Radesky, Christakis,Moreno& Cross, 2016). The modern school curriculum is designed in such a way that it fully incorporates making the use of technology and multimedia in the education process. A complete transformation has been witnessed in the mostly developing countries as their primary and secondary education is not confined to traditional classrooms alone. The increasing growth of ICT tools has increased in our schools and has become a reality. Use of Mobile technology is growing worldwide with a broad range of users, including students from all levels of education. The use of social media via mobile phones is mushrooming in all educational institutes and among all levels of students. The students are using social media for a variety of purposes chatting, sharing and uploading the educational content as well. However, most of the studies have shown that using mobile phones in the early stages of your school can have negative consequences on the intellectual capacity in the long run. Modern generations of children growsup in the environment where they have an early access to play computer games and other technological devices resulted in the development of different attitudes.

1.2. Use of Mobile Technologies in higher Education

Mobile devices have occupied a significant place in the lives of common people as well as among students. In higher education, students use this technology for information access and to establish connections with others. Undoubtedly, an increasing growth of digital technologies in twenty years has been on the anvil and in the economically advanced and developed countries, the use of mobile technology among adults has also increased and they have accumulated a huge amount of technology experience before entering higher educational setup. Mobile learning, over the years, has had an effective impact and has become an important component in higher education as it makes it possible for students to learn, communicate collaborate, and share ideas among each other with the aid of internet and or wireless technology. A survey in the united states established that, 8–18yearold spent daily 4 to 5 hours on ICT devices outside schools using them for messaging, talking to peers, watching educational videos etc. (Rideout, Foehr& Roberts, *2010*). The role of teachers in the modern educational has shifted a great way- to be a supporter, mediator and guide etc. The teachers in the higher education must use technology for the good of the students. Other new facets in the technology- Web 2.0, use are highly becoming the essential parts of higher education students. Web 2.0 tools will ensure the flexibility and greater audiences in order to engage the students in the teaching learning process as compared to the fixed PCs in the labs which hinder their learning process as they are available only during the working hours of the institution.

Adults in China, and Korea usedmobile technologies to establish connections with each other and on the contrary, the adults in America were using mobile technologies to access and retrieve information related to their academic works (Wang, Ran &Salvendy, *2011*). The education and learning process of the unprivileged sections in the society can have a positive impact if mobile technologies are integrated with education. In developing nations also, cell phones with internet connection can have a higher impact on the education of the students (Kumar et al., 2010*)*. Day in and day out the younger population is excessively make use of MT. Mobile technologies facilitate the users in different dimensions; from educational use to social interaction to show off the talent to advertising their businesses. *In libraries* the users having access to mobile technologies are experiencing great changes today as compared to somewhat 15 years ago. Both Academic and Non Academic libraries response are using mobile technology to make the user experience a good one. In case of libraries, the online catalogues of the libraries/ OPACs (Online Public Access Catalogs) are can be used and accessed on any device, 24*7 via smartphones and other digital gadgets. Moreover, *e-books* can be offered to those patrons who are using mobile technologies.

CONCLUSION

Mobile technologies have become increasingly prevalent and inescapable facet of people in the modern era and have some spectacular benefits associated with them. Mobile technologies have been at the forefront at making the information readily available to users at their convenience time and place i.e. users can have the look at the current or required information at homes/ offices etc. It has been at the heart of higher educational institutions all across the globe to realize the potential and power of implementing MTs to provide easy access to the learning. Undoubtedly, a large population of students is left out due to the shortage of vacancies and infrastructure in the higher educational institutions. One of the solutions to these shortcomings is to integrate mobile technology with the education, so that the adequate as well as equal benefits will be received by the students of all communities. For libraries to stay relevant to the diverse demands of the clients, they need to make serious efforts to make library services compatible with the mobile technology. With this the users will have the user friendly and personalized library services on their screens.

REFERENCES

Ashford, R. (2010). QR codes and academic libraries: Reaching mobile users. *College & Research Libraries News, 71*(10), 526–530. https://doi.org/10.5860/crln.71.10.8454

Buarki, H. J., & Dar, S. A. (2019). Anytime, anywhere access to information resources: A case study from Kuwait. *Library Hi Tech News, 36*(7), 20–24. https://doi.org/10.1108/LHTN-08-2019-0049

Chassiakos, Y. L. R., Radesky, J., Christakis, D., Moreno, M. A., & Cross, C. (2016). Children and adolescents and digital media. *Pediatrics, 138*(5), e20162593.

Dar, S. A. (2019). Mobile library initiatives: A new way to revitalize the academic library settings. *Library Hi Tech News, 36*(5), 15–21. https://doi.org/10.1108/LHTN-05-2019-0032

Hamad, F., Tbaishat, D., & Al-Fadel, M. (2017). The role of social networks in enhancing the library profession and promoting academic library services: A comparative study of the University of Jordan and Al-Balqaa' Applied University. *Journal of Librarianship and Information Science, 49*(4), 397–408. https://doi.org/10.1177/0961000616656043

Huang, Y.-M., Pu, Y.-H., Chen, T.-S., & Chiu, P.-S. (2015). Development and evaluation of the mobile library service system success model: A case study of Taiwan. *The Electronic Library, 33*(6), 1174–1192. https://doi.org/10.1108/EL-06-2014-0094

Jharotia, A. K. (2015). Mobile Applications and Technologies for Libraries: An Overview. *Digital India-Digital Libraries.* Presented at the Knowledge Organisation in Academic Libraries, Manipal University Jaipur, India.

Khan, A. I., Al-Shihi, H., Al-Khanjari, Z. A., & Sarrab, M. (2015). Mobile Learning (M-Learning) adoption in the Middle East: Lessons learned from the educationally advanced countries. *Telematics and Informatics, 32*(4), 909-920.

Kumar, A., Tewari, A., Shroff, G., Chittamuru, D., Kam, M. & Canny, J. (2010). An exploratory study of unsupervised mobile learning in Rural India. *In Proceedings of ACM Conference on Human Factors in Computing Systems (CHI'10)*, Atlanta, Georgia, April 10–15, 2010 Best Paper Honorable Mention. Retrieved from *http://www.millee.org/*

Law, R., Chan, I. C. C., & Wang, L. (2018). A comprehensive review of mobile technology use in hospitality and tourism. *Journal of Hospitality Marketing & Management, 27*(6), 626–648. https://doi.org/10.1080/19368623.2018.1423251

Mansouri, A., & Soleymani Asl, N. (2019). Assessing mobile application components in providing library services. *The Electronic Library, 37*(1), 49–66. https://doi.org/10.1108/EL-10-2018-0204

Mayisela, T. (2013). The potential use of mobile technology: Enhancing accessibility and communication in a blended learning course. *South African Journal of Education, 33*(1), 1–18. https://doi.org/10.15700/saje.v33n1a629

Mir, M. M. ud in, & Kumar, S. (2015). Evolution of Mobile Wireless Technology from 0G to 5G. *International Journal of Computer Science and Information Technologies, 6*(3), 2545–2551.

Rideout, V. J., Foehr, U. G.&Roberts, D. F. (2010). *Generation M2: media in the lives of 8 to 18 year olds. Menlo Park, CA: Henry J. Kaiser Family Foundation. Retrieved March 1, 2013, from http://www.kff.org/entmedia/upload/8010.pd*

Routet, J. F., Levonen, J., & Biardeau, A. (2001). *Multimedia learning cognitive and instructional issues.* Oxford: Elsevier Science Ltd.

Roy, M. B. (2017). *APPLICATION OF MOBILE TECHNOLOGY IN LIBRARY SERVICES.* 5.

Unhelkar, B. (Ed.). (2009). *Handbook of Research in Mobile Business, Second Edition: Technical, Methodological and Social Perspectives.* https://doi.org/10.4018/978-1-60566-156-8

Wang, L., Ran, P. P. R., & Salvendy, G. (2011). A cross-culture study on older adults in information technology acceptance. *International Journal of Mobile Communication, 9*(5), 421–440.

Wang, X., Li, J., Yang, M., Chen, Y., & Xu, X. (2018). An empirical study on the factors influencing mobile library usage in IoT era. *Library Hi Tech, 36*(4), 605–621. https://doi.org/10.1108/LHT-01-2018-0008.

2

Application of Radio-frequency Identification (RFID) Technology in Library and Information Centers

INTRODUCTION

Libraries have so far always been keen to accept and adopt new scientific technological innovation in order to make its service more organized, save time, bring perfection and accuracy and at the same time to reduce manual workload. This habit or tendency keeps the library and information centers alive and relevant with time.

Theradio-frequency identification(RFID) technology, in the same way as we see or the other, came in to use during World War II (1940s) by the military persons for identifying their aircrafts or other various military purposes. Later its' commercial application was observed in the early 1980s and within two subsequent decades it gained a wide application in several activities, such as;

collecting toll taxes in USA, Italy, France, Norway and Portugal, in manufacturing industries to trace their accessories, vehicles, parts etc., in nuclear research centers and also in animal raring or cattle tracking. But now, it has a very wide applicability and it is rapidly spreading worldwide irrespective of developed, developing and under-developed countries or regions(Jones et al., 2005).

Although, RFID (Radio Frequency Identification) came in to reality in 1940s but it was first patented by Mario E. Cardullo, an American inventor, for inventing RFID tag with read-write (re-writable) memory on January 23, 1973 and its present standard, combination of automation and well security mechanism with for well maintenance of library materials, presented in 2001 (Rajanarayana et al., 2015).

Due to the vast role of RFID in identification and tracking of an item, it is now more or less used in every field, including libraries. In our day-to-day life, we witness RFID is exercised in controlling the delivery of goods and automobiles', to control traffic on the high-ways, to collect taxes, for the management of parking areas automatically, for 'vehicle access control, in the premises of airports, rail-stations, ski lifting and many more (Dwivedi et al., 2013).

WHAT IS RFID?

RFID is a part of the Automatic Identification and Data Capture (AIDC) technology family,contains barcode and smart card as well. RFID is a wireless device based on radio frequency and microchip technology which in use of electromagnetic wave to transfer data in view of instinctive identification as well as tracking of tags attached to objects. "*RFID-based technology captures data from an object without physical contact and possible wear and associated damage to both reader and receiver. RFID is one of the most technologies being adopted by both industry and academic world"* (Smith, 2005, p16). RFID is a mechanism which works based on electromagnetic radio waves to read the coded information inserted in the tag. The tag is connected with an antenna; again antenna is connected to the server. In this way, all the parts of entire RFID system are connected to each other to form a well network connectivity to perform works eloquently.

According to Automatic Identification and Data Capture (AIDC),

> *"Radio Frequency identification is a technology that uses radio waves to transfer data between a reader and an electronic tag which is attached to a particular object. Typical uses are for object identification and tracking" (Miller, 2013)*

According to Harrods's Librarians' Glossary and Reference Book,

> *"Radio Frequency Identification, an alternative to the Bar Code that uses tiny microchips in tags to hold and transmit detailed data about the item tagged. RFID has advantages over bar codes such as the ability to hold more data, the ability to change the stored data as processing occurs, it does not require line-of-sight to transfer data and is very effective in harsh environments where bar code labels may not work" (Prytherch, 2005, 602).*

WHY RFID IN LIBRARY?

RFID is one of those newly emerging and sound technologies which are being adopted in multiple sectors all around the world, for example; business, manufacturing, defense, academic cum library. As we all know, library is a system/place where millions and millions books, periodicals, manuscripts, gray-literature, newspapers, CDs, DVDs, microfilms, microfiches and many other e-resources are stored and maintained. For a librarian, it is a huge challenge to keep the library services in motion with maintaining its' resources and library decorum. In this regard, RFID is a revolutionary innovation for library automation to make the librarians as well as end users bit happier.

As Chelliah et al.,(2015) mentioned;

> *"[RFID] this oldest new technology' creates potential for staff to develop and implement innovative methods for inventory, circulating and tracking library objects that accommodate far higher volume and speed and involve a strong focus on improved library services"p.114*

In their quest to serve the patrons in the possible easiest and organised way, libraries have always been at the forefront to adopt emerging and advanced technologies one after another since decades after decades.RFID technology is used in library due to its very nature of library automation, which helps the libraries to manage its resources in effective way. It also has features to provide an enhanced quality of services including identification of wrongly shelved books, missing books, reducing theft of books, advanced security characteristics, inventory accuracy, and self-issue-return of books.

COMPONENTS OF RFID TECHNOLOGY

The system RFID is a family of various small technologies; all these parts together make RFID as worthy system. These components are;

RFID tags

Readers or Sensors

Antenna

Server

RFID Label Printer

Handheld Reader

Self-Issue and Return Station

Drop Box

RFID Smart Card

1. Tag : It is heart of RFID mechanism, is generally attached with inside of the back-cover of book or onto the CDs, DVs etc. The tag is arrayed with electronically programmed tiny chip and a small antenna to connect with server.

These tags are smart labels of thin paper that programmed with certain information. This tiny chip, integrated inside the tag, is the communicator between the tag and RFID reader with the help of antenna and server by creating radio frequency wave. RFID tags which are normally available in market are categorized into three types; active, semi-active, passive and semi-passive (Mehrjerdi, 2011). Again these are categorized under three groups; read only, WROM and read/write or re-write (Pandey & Mahajan, 2010). In a very simplified way, 'read only' tags are where coding of unique information is done at the time of manufacturing. Hence, this kind of tags are unable to rewrite on the other hand, WROM tags such a type of tag where unique information is coded and programmed by the stakeholders and unable to rewrite further. While, read/write (re-write) tags are those where programmed information can be modified whenever it is required. As a matter of simplicity and stakeholders friendly, libraries do prefer these kinds of tags.

2. Readers : A RFID reader, eyes of RFID device, is subsumes of antenna, receiver, transmitter and decoder. Reader makes communication with tag and identifies the objects by decoding the coded information programmed in the tag. As soon as reader enters into the arena of radio frequency wave, it connected antenna and detects the item by decoding the information. Usually, when this device is used inside the premises is known as reader and if it is exercised at the entry or exit points of the premises are known as sensors.

3. Antenna : An antenna, nerves of RFID mechanism, is connecting nod between the tag and RFID reader to decode and identify an item. This antenna has a crucial role in making radio wave and to make the alarm active. Because, antenna produces radio frequency with whom RFID reader connected to read the programmed information. Therefore, antennas are communicating channels in between tag and reader in the process of communication.

4. Server : It is the brain of entire Radio Frequency Identification device. All the organs of RFID system are directly/indirectly connected with this server. Just like the function of human brain, it receives information from reader/sensor and transmits it to the circulation or respective database of the library. Nowadays, the different softwares which are in functioning with server are (Session Initiation Protocol) SIP/SIP2, (Application Programming Interface) APIs and NCIP/SLNP to communicate with concerned library software (Pandey & Mahajan, 2010).

5. RFID Label Printer : RFID label printer has categorically been designed for writing information onto RFID chips implanted in smart labels. It consist a radio frequency encoder, that transfer the information to the chip and encodes it. The printer is used to print the smart labels with a barcode or any different form of programmed information.

6. Handheld Reader : It is a kind of reader which is known as Handheld Reader, used to read the items/ documents on the library book shelves. It is able to read the items from a certain distance means there is no need of touching them. It is verily used for searching of wrongly shelved books (stock rectification) and in stock verification as well. Indeed, it saves the times and manpower to exercise the searching and stock verification in library (Pandey & Mahajan, 2010).

7. Self-Issue and Return Station : RFID enabled

libraries offer special services to its end users, for example, ability to check-out and check-in the issued items of the library resources by themselves. Users need to scan their ID card to active their respective account and then the items, they want to be issued or returned, have to be kept on the kiosk follow certain simple steps like ATM machine.

8. Drop Box : It is a very special facility rendered by the libraries with the help of RFID to the users. The patrons can return their issued items even if the library is closed. Patrons need to drop the items into it. The system will automatically find out the name of the users on whom it was issued and information of the book. Once the process is over, system will provide a slip with brief information about the items.

9. Smart Card : Smart Card is like an ordinary ID card, ATM Card, Debit or Credit Card which is blending of various technologies. Integrated Circuit chip is embedded on it. It has a capability of 100 times more retaining of information than the other magnetic stripe card. Smart card is of two types; Contact card and Contactless cards. According to (Abiodun, 2017)

> *"A smart card is a card with a microchip embedded in it. The card is similar in size and shape to a plastic credit card. These cards take the form of either 'contact' cards that require a card reader or 'contact less' cards which use radio frequency signals to operate. The embedded chip however empowers the card to be useful in a variety of environments"* P. 2

SMART CARD: ITS SALIENT FEATURES

1. It provides speedy and easy way to authenticate the identity of a stakeholder or objects.
2. It offers more security and harder to alter with than bar code.

3. They can hoard a larger amount of data and also can separate those data into a multi-partition file system, so that different activities can securely run on a single card.
4. They can control who has access to files on the card as well as in a computer network.
5. They are also being used in biometrics for complete security purpose.
6. Smart card can be developed in view of their own cryptographic algorithm.
7. It can accommodate with all kind upgradation and latest technologies without changing the standard thirty nine bar code or the three tracks, high energy stripe systems etc.

APPLICATION OF RFID AND SMART CARD IN LIBRARIES

According to the study, there are more than five hundred thousand RFID systems installed in library worldwide. The study further confirmed that Singapore Public Library was found to the first library to implement RFID system with complete features in the year 1998 (Singh & Mahajan, 2014). Since then, the use of RFID in libraries has grown up drastically. Now, with the help of this radio identification device library has become possible to those works within days which earlier used to take months. Besides it, users are able to issue-return and check their account, required items by themselves. More importantly, libraries have become more capable to control missing/losing of books.

RFID Tag : It is typically a thin paper, smart label, flexible and nearly 2"*2" in size. Generally, this tag is affixed unremarkably on the verso of the title page of inside of the back cover of book. RFID tag contains a small antenna and a very tiny chip that store certain information in a coded form.

SELF-CHECK-OUT STATION

The Self-Check-out station or self-issue kiosk is a computer aided automatic checking out machine like an ATM machine with a touch display and RFID reader, software for users' data identification, document verification and circulation of tagged materials. It allows the user to borrow the reading resources without the help of library staff. The users have to enter their smart card into it and machine will identify the respective user and the validity of the card. Then the user will be able to issue the documents whichever he/she wants to check out, the status of each documents are updated automatically on the concerned database and users will get a slip of checked out documents just like the transection slip in ATM machine. Hence, the patrons can borrow the documents by their own without taking any help from library staff (Singh & Mahajan, 2014).

BOOK-DROP (CHECK-IN STATION)

It is a box like machine where RFID chip is attached inside its wall. Here patrons can return or check-in their issued documents by themselves without the assistance of library staff like check out process. The users need to drop off their documents gently which they want into it; the drop box will automatically verify and identify the documents and the patrons on whom it was issued as well. After the completing of this process the patrons will get a slip about the details of this activity. The most attractive point is that the patrons can complete this process even when library is closed. The book-drop machine can be installed anywhere, not necessarily around the library premises, for example; hostel campuses, near bank, rail stations, and shopping malls.

EXIT SENSORS

The exit sensor is fitted at the entrance or exit point of library in a rectangular shaped vertical frame through which the users can make entry or exit. This is fitted mainly for two purposes in the library, one for item identification and another is for antitheft purpose. An (Electronic Article Surveillance) EAS system is used by libraries. If the document is not properly checked-out then an alarm will activate. Another is on *theft*; it plays a very significant role in order to theft detection or to reduce the theft activity, which is a fundamental feature of the chip in the interior RFID tag.

AUTOMATED SORTING STATION

This is a very advanced and assisting feature of RFID. The items which have been returned or checked-in by the users are sorted by this automated sorted station. After sorting items are re-shelved on the actual location. It saves the time and manual efforts as well (Singh & Mahajan, 2014).

APPLICATION SOFTWARE

Application software is needed to run the RFID system properly, particularly, to transmit the programmed information whatever is stored onto the tag. Software helps to make a linkage among the organs of RFID. When RFID reader reads an item, the data goes to server and with the help of software; server's response goes to the respective library automation software in time. Not only this, but every functions of RFID become possible due to application software, without it System will not work.

RFID SMART CARD

This card is used for making different activities in RFID based libraries like check in and checks out. This card is being used for many other purposes in the same libraries like staff attendance and leaf. In simple words we can say it is now used for biometric technologies for security purposes (Chaurasia, 2014)

ADVANTAGES OF RFID FOR LIBRARIES

Every single entity especially new technology has two aspects i.e., positive and negative no matter when it came, where it came and why it came? RFID is not exception of it. It also has advantages and some challenges as well. Indeed, positive points have an edge over the other. Here about the advantages of RFID some of the points are given below;

(Smith, 2005) has mentioned:

> *"RFID is a means of capturing data about an object without using a human to read and recode the data. Radio frequency (RF) tracking is a current and highly beneficial technological advance that could lead to serious cost reduction in the future for all retailers"p.17*

1. Accuracy : RFID device will be able to give accurate and specific information about each and every specific item, where it is or who has the item, in real time.

2. Alarm : If a document or item is missing, misplaced or taken out of the library or building, it will alarm.

3. Compatibility : RFID application is now easily available for all major operating systems such as Windows, IOS, Linux/Ubuntu and Android (Smart Phone).

4. Automatic Circulation : RFID enables users to issue-return, check availability their required items and patrons' profile checking by their own without the intervention of library staff.

5. Book Drop : It has book drop facility which provides users an ultimate opportunity to return their issued materials at any time without going to the library circulation point, no matter whether library is opened or closed.

6. Reduce Workload : It plays a significant role to reduce the clerical and monotonous work-load in library and information centers.

7. Stock Verification/Rectification : Stock verification and rectification services were supposed to be a very time consuming and annoying work. Every staff wanted to avoid this irritating job but RFID has made this stock verification and stock rectification very easy and time saving.

8. Security : Librarians are always concern about the missing and losing of library materials no matter what type of library. In this context, RFID has become a savior up to the certain extent to the librarians due to its ability to identify and alarm at the un-checked out materials. It helps to reduce the theft activities.

9. Standard : After all, this device (RFID) provides a standard to the library services and helps the libraries to reach into a new height.

CHALLENGES OF RFID SYSTEM

1. Costly Setup : The main and foremost challenge of installing a RFID in a library is its high price. Due to its high price, many libraries, despite of having wish/desire of RFID, unable to install it. Particularly, small library or public library where budget is a main concern to the librarians or stakeholders.

2. Removal of Tags : Most of the cases, the tags are fixed to the inner side of the back cover of the books and generally that is visible to all. Hence, there is chance, and it is happening in many times, of removing or taking off these tags by the misbehavior of some users. Once if the tags are removed then entire RFID system becomes futile.

3. Sensor Problems : Sometimes, what happens if a un-check out library materials keeping are taken out of library premises and any gadget such as mobile phones are kept inside the book then alarm of the sensor gate does not work.

4. Uniformity in Tags : There is another challenge which libraries are facing is when library change their RFID vendor due to some reasons and reach out a new vendor in this case libraries are said to retagging of entire materials. This happens due to lacking of uniformity of tags and coding of information inside the tags.

5. Infrastructure : Infrastructure is another important hindrance of RFID implementing in many libraries. As far as public library and libraries of colleges and schools are concerned in developing and under-develop countries, their infrastructure is somewhere compromising.

DIFFERENCE BETWEEN BARCODE, ELECTROMAGNETIC STRIP AND RFID

As we have discussed repeatedly that RFID technology is the more advance from different angles. So here, it will be better to draw a comparative picture among them, so that we can understand how it is better and more helpful.

Subject	*Barcode*	*Electromagnetic Strip*	*RFID*
Line of Sight	For scanning barcode a straight Line of sight is required	There is no need of straight Line of sight	RFID Reader can read it with the help of radio wave, no need of line of sight
Number of Item	Only on item can be scanned by the scanner at a time	More than one items can be read and scanned	It can read and scan multiple items at single point of time
Time	Comparatively more time required to read a barcode	Comparatively lesser time required to read a barcode	Very less time required to read a barcode
Memory	Barcode does not have such	It also does not have Read/write	RFID has Read/Write

	Read/write memory	memory	memory
Human intervention	To read a barcode human intervention is required	To read it human intervention is not needed	To read it no human intervention is required
Visibility	Barcode should be visible to be scanned	No need of visibility	It can be inserted on any nonmetallic item
Manipulation	There is a chance of barcode manipulation	There is no chance of magnetic strip manipulation	There is no chance at all, since it is based on Radio wave
Chance of damage	Barcode can be un-cleared/ blurred due to some reasons	There is no chance of ambiguity or blurred	No chance of damage/ blurred
Durability	Durability of barcode is lesser than the Magnetic strips and RFID	Its durability is lesser than RFID but more than barcode	It has a very long durability
Read Range	The read range is very less	Read range is more than barcode	Read range is more than Barcode and magnetic strips
Storage Capacity	Minimum capacity to hold data	Lesser capacity of hold data as compare to RFID	Capacity of holding data is more than the others
Cost	It is cheap	Bit expensive	Expensive
Security	Security is no very high	Comparatively higher security	Very high security

Vendors : Worldwide, there are so many vendors who are working on it and provide necessary assistance to the stakeholders on demand basis. In India, 3M, Libsys, Bibliotheca, VTLS, Checkpoint, InfoTech, X-ident and Vernon etc. are some of the popular vendors.

Future of RFID in Libraries

Although the use of RFID started in 1990s but now the concept of implementing of RFID in libraries is echoing everywhere. Therefore, number of RFID implemented libraries in India or abroad areincreasing rapidly. Presently, numbers of RFID manufacturing agents are available and they are working hard in keeping it at lower price, which amplified the number of RFID implemented libraries. In developed countries, USA, Canada, Germany, France, England, Australia, New Zealand, Portugal etc. the scenario of RFID based library is very common and feasible here and there. But in developing countries like India the picture is very different. However, now trends are changing and plenty of libraries are start using of it, for example, IIT Kharagpur, IIT Delhi, IIT Madras, IIT Mandi, IIT Roorkee, IIT Patna, IISc Bangalore, Gautam Buddha University, Greater Noida, Amity University Noida, IIT Gandhinagar, Pondicherry University, Punjab University, IIM Lucknow, NIT Rourkela, NIT Surat, IIM Shillong, Punjabi University, University of Jammu, University of Kashmir, University of Pune, Parliament library, New Delhi, KIIT Bhuvneshwar, India Law University Delhi. Apart from these, many more libraries are using partially or are in initial purpose (Singh & Mahajan, 2014).

CONCLUSION

No doubt, RFID system is one of the latest, advanced, reliable and secure technologies in libraries as well as in commercial sector also. It reduces the physical efforts and increases reliability, accuracy effectiveness simultaneously for different activities as we mentioned earlier. Most important is that it reduces the most precious thing of the user that is time. We have also seen that future prospect of this technology is very bright and its acceptance is increasing at a tremendous rate, though, high cost is its main obstacle for the medium and small organization to install it. Very surely it's also have advantages and disadvantages as we have already seen instead of this we can say this system or technology brings a revolution in terms of library's clerical and hectic jobs. At the end, it can be said that hopefully technologist will keep in mind the drawbacks of this subset systems so that it can be more usable and acceptable by all kinds of libraries.

REFERENCES

Abiodun, A. (2017). *Card Based Security in Library (Smart Card Technology* (Pp. 1–14). Retrieved From School Of Scienceand Technology &'" Gateway Polytechnic website: https://www.academia.edu/33303303/CARD_BASED_SECURITY_IN_LIBRARY_SMART_CARD_TECHNOLOGY

Chaurasia, N. (2014). *Emerging technologies for library management and services*. New Delhi: Ess Ess Publications.

Chelliah, J., Sood, S., & Scholfield, S. (2015). Realising the strategic value of RFID in academic libraries: A case study of the University of Technology Sydney. *The Australian Library Journal, 64*(2), 113–127. https://doi.org/10.1080/00049670.2015.1013005

Dwivedi, Y. K., Kapoor, K. K., Williams, M. D., & Williams, J. (2013). RFID systems in libraries: An empirical examination of factors affecting system use and user satisfaction. *International Journal of Information Management, 33*(2), 367–377. https://doi.org/10.1016/j.ijinfomgt.2012.10.008

Jones, P., Hillier, D., & Comfort, D. (2005). The benefits, challenges and impacts of radio frequency identification technology (RFID) for retailers in the UK. *Marketing Intelligence & Planning, 23*(4), 395–402. https://doi.org/10.1108/02634500510603492

Miller, J. (2013, September 4). What is Automatic Identification and Data Capture (AIDC)? - AB&R (American Barcode and RFID). Retrieved December 27, 2019, from AB&R website: https://www.abr.com/automatic-identification-and-data-capture-aidc/

Pandey, D. P., & Mahajan, K. D. (2010). *Application of RFID Technology in Libraries and Role of Librarian*. 7. Jaipur.

Prytherch, R. J. (2005). *Harrod's librarians' glossary and reference book: A directory of over 10,200 terms, organizations, projects and acronyms in the areas of information management, library science, publishing and archive management.* Retrieved from http://site.ebrary.com/id/10343276

Rajanarayana, M., Sasikala, B., & Geethavani, B. (2015). A Review on RFID Technology and Applications. *International Journal Of Engineering And Computer Science, 7*(6), 4099–24105.

Singh, N. K., & Mahajan, P. (2014). RFID and It's Use in Libraries: A Literature Review. *International Journal of Information Dissemination and Technology, 4*(2), 8.

Smith, A. D. (2005). Exploring radio frequency identification technology and its impact on business systems. *Information Management & Computer Security, 13*(1), 16–28. https://doi.org/10.1108/09685220510582647

Zare Mehrjerdi, Y. (2011). RFID: The big player in the libraries of the future. *The Electronic Library, 29*(1), 36–51. https://doi.org/10.1108/02640471111111424

3

Web 2.0 and Library 2.0

The term Web 2.0 made its debut in 1999 and gained immense popularity in the early 2000s.Other terms that are used for Web 2.0 are "participatory web, collaborative web or web as platform". Web 2.0 includes a wide range of web formats blogs, social networking sites- Facebook, YouTube, Instagram, Flicker, RSS, Weebly, Digg, My Space, streaming media, tagging, folksonomies and Wikipedia etc. The second generation of Web, often called as "Web 2.0/Participatory or Collaborative web" and its diverse applications have created new and diverse opportunities and ways to share and disseminate information across lines. Moreover, these tools can be labelled as "collaborative Internet applications". The coming of Web 2.0 has completely transformed the ways the internet users used to generate, use of upload information on the Web.

VARIOUS DEFINITIONS OF WEB 2.0

"Web 2.0, term devised to differentiate the post-dotcom bubble World Wide Web with its emphasis on social networking, content generated by users, and cloud computing from that which came before. The 2.0 appellation is used in analogy with common computer software naming conventions to indicate a new, improved version". (Encyclopedia Britannica)

According to Berners-Lee, "Web 2.0...means using the standards which have been produced by all these people working on Web 1.0. So, Web 2.0...means moving some of the thinking client side so making it more immediate, but the idea of the Web as interaction between people is really what the Web is. That was what it was designed to be as a collaborative space where people can interact".

"Web2.0 tools to illuminate three key characteristics of the Web2.0 platform: (a) user-initiated publishing of information without significant technical knowledge, (b) social networking, and (c) online communities formed around specific content" (Rosen & Nelson, 2008).

Stephens and Collins (2007) view Web 2.0 as "the next incarnation of the World Wide Web, where digital tools allow users to create, change, and publish dynamic content of all kinds... to make connections, carry on conversations, and collaborate" (p. 253). Furthermore, they distill "Web 2.0 principles to: a)Conversations: User participation, discussion and feedback are welcomed and encouraged, b)Community: Open conversations can lead to a sense of community and belonging c)Participation: New information is created via collaboration between users d)Experience: Engagement with other users and the community is rewarding and provides some type of fulfillment e)Sharing: Users can contribute as much or as little as they like"(p.253).

With the emergence of Web 2.0, a grand new shift has been witnessed, how people use and view Internet. It allows even an ordinary user to participate in the consumption or production (both creation and modification) of the content over the internet.

WEB 2.0 TOOLS

Web 2.0 has given a new shape how internet was

used in the Web 1.0 era. The internet pages in the Web 1.0 period were mostly static and user have had a less control over the content available on internet, while in case of web 2.0, the user can modify and edit the content. To put in simpler words, in Web 2.0 users not only read, but create information. As there is now centralized power that controls the web so web permits users to use and reuse the content in new ways Web 2.0 tools can be seen as the interactive digital platforms with multipurpose features that one can use for sharing, creating and uploading any type of content online almost free of cost. Web 2.0 platforms are very easy to use and can also be used to share the collaborative works. As stated earlier one of the most outstanding hallmarks of Web 2.0 tools/ websites is their ease of use. A little or no time is consumed while one wants to find his/her required content that suits his /her information needs. Other benefits of these web 2.0 is they are highly user-friendly. The content shared or posted on these sites can be easily verified for their validity, objectivity and authenticity and perhaps that is why these sites are number 1 choice for the most of Web 2.0 users. User-generated content and interactivity are the fundamentals of all Web 2.0 applications (O'Reilly, 2005).

LIBRARY 2.0

Libraries have a vital role to play in the development of societies and in the technology driven world. The role of libraries has been challenged but it provides ample opportunities to employ these technological changes to serve their missions and purposes. Libraries have been rendering their services since a very long time and have played an important role to engage and allow people to have access to information resources. Keeping in view the growth in modern technologies, the modern libraries over the past three decades or so have been redefined, as lot has changed ever since they have adopted technological reforms in them. Now a days they are seen as the places where one gets access to variety of information sources of his choice and time in different formats found feasible by the clients. In the modern times, the term such as library without walls, virtual library, hybrid library, digital library, cloud libraries have come into force. 20th century saw an important milestone in the library development such as introduction of integrated library systems (ILS), a shift from card to online catalogues allowing clients to search the library resources from anywhere. Undoubtedly, in the past two decades a drastic technological developments took place, and libraries were no longer hesitant to adopt and apply these technological developments in making their overall functioning structure a better one. In the presence of Web 2.0 environment the concept "Library 2.0" came into exist.

The term "Library 2.0" was coined by librarian Michael Casey in September 2005. Whenever a new technology emerges or is developed the concerned people start to talk about its relevance, adoption, implementing the same in their institutions. One of the fundamentals of adopting Library 2.0 revolves round users i.e. user-centered change is always eminent while adopting this generation of technology in the libraries. This will help libraries in the continuous in achieving the purposeful changes while accepting the feedback of their users related the services they offer. Feedback from the users can help libraries to offer best services from time to time which will help in eliminating the barriers faced by both sides while delivering or using the library services.

Wallis (2007) defined Library 2.0 as "the combination of Web 2.0 and libraries, together with the libraries' traditions of serving users". Lankes*et al.* (2007) defines the concept as "an attempt to apply Web 2.0 technologies to the purpose of the library, together with goals for greater community involvement".

"Library 2.0 is a model of library service that includes constant and purposeful change and user participation in the creation and maintenance of services, while maintaining a primary goal of extending the library's reach to potential library users. Implementing a system of change and participation will enable you to expand your user base and reach those customers you previously have not been able to reach. This model also calls for libraries to keep up with rapidly changing technology, social trends, and customer expectations, something libraries must do to remain relevant. Although these concepts of change and user involvement are not necessarily new, using them together in a Library 2.0 environment will help you keep your library relevant in the wake of the rapidly changing needs of your customers" (Casey & Savastinuk,2007).

It empowers users through participatory, user driven services; the main reason to adopt web 2.0 services is to enhance the services and procedures in the library. "It is the ongoing response to Web 2.0, a participatory, networked, interactive, and collaborative community of web users. Library 2.0 is the shorthand for a vast array of initiatives in all types of libraries to incorporate the tools for online collaboration into new ways to deliver effective library services" (ALA,2019). Library 2.0 enables the users and institutions to make use of web 2.0 tools in the library settings making them highly user-centered. The important aspect of Library 2.0 is relevant to institutions/libraries who want to provide their services to the off-campus students which enable the off-campus users to make use of library services 24*7. So, library 2.0 encourages on one hand the collaboration, on the other hand user contribution.

Maness (2006) highlights that Library 2.0 is the combination of four important elements:

(a) User-Centered : It is users who are involved in the creation of the content and services they view within the library's web-presence, OPAC, etc. "The consumption and creation of content is dynamic, and thus the roles of librarian and user are not always clear b) multi-media experience: both the collections and services of Library 2.0 contain video and audio components. While this is not often cited as a function of Library 2.0, it is here suggested that it should be. c) socially rich: The library's web-presence includes users' presences. There are both synchronous (e.g. IM) and asynchronous (e.g. wikis) ways for users to communicate with one another and with librarians. d)Communally innovative: This is perhaps the single most important aspect of Library 2.0. It rests on the foundation of libraries as a community service, but understands that as communities change, libraries must not only change with them, and they must allow users to change the library. It seeks to continually change its services, to find new ways to allow communities, not just individuals to seek, find, and utilize information". The functions of Library 2.0 may not be confined to searching, but it must include the finding; not only about access to the housed resources but should also involve sharing the same. Simply, Library 2.0 lays great emphasis on building communities and establishing the collaborative environments for the masses for the purpose not only to use but to create and share the information. Libraries over the years have implemented various technological reforms in order to extend their services and access to information sources to the diverse user groups of different ages.

Blogs and Libraries

As per the Wikipedia definition "blog or often called Weblog is a discussion or informational website published on the World Wide Web consisting of discrete, often informal diary-style text entries (posts). Posts are typically displayed in reverse chronological order, so that the most recent post appears first, at the top of the web page". It is a software tool which allows the internet users to create the websites easily. It is a website or platform where a person or group of persons can share their views on a particular topic or subject. The fundamental aim of writing blogs is to connect with your audience (customers/users). Blogs are now widely used by businesses both profit and non-profit, educational institutions etc. "Blogs offer an avenue for delivering that value to a global audience. They provide a hub for tutorials and walk-throughs, and an avenue for crafting and constructing resources that help individuals that are looking for useful information" (Forbes,2017). While some blogs are public they offer one to post comments and offer feedback and these help the people to actively engage with the community.

ADVANTAGES OF BLOGGING

Blogs help improve communication and writing skills.

Blogs can become a source of income.

Blogs can be used to develop and strengthen relationships with existing and new customers.

Blogs allows an individual to establish himself an expert in the relevant field.

Blogging helps individuals to become digitally literate.

Blogs can be used promote businesses both profit

and non-profit nature.

Blogs act as a great source of information.

The advantages blogs carry with them is they can be easily maintained and updated on regular intervals and continuously forcing and allowing librarians and users to remain up to date but the main obstacle remains the readerships numbers. Marketing of services remains one of the core objectives of every library to sensitize the defined population about the functions and services these libraries offer to their clients. In the old times, libraries used to marketize their services by making use of newspapers, magazines, TV ads and radio announcements. Information professionals may employ and use blogs for the variety of purposes i.e. progress reports of libraries, post book reviews, list of services offered/new service, new arrivals, stats about usage of library collection by users, announcing the new or coming library events. Attracting new patrons and interacting with the community of library users- blogs largely fulfills the task. Employing blogs can help librarians to receive a continuous feedback and if they are willing, they can invite them to the discussion forums. In other words, it may be said that blogs act as a newsletter for libraries while diminishing the cost of printed copies and avoids more time consumption for reaching the particular resource to the required client.

WIKIS AND LIBRARIES

Wikis are open, dynamic software applications/ websites where information knowledge is collaboratively share and uploaded and can be free to use by any user. Another Web 2.0 tools- Wikis can be put to use by libraries to support a variety of activities in any type of library. Over the years they have emerged powerful web 2.0 tools platforms in improving the connection and collaboration between library staff and their clients. When wikis are used by libraries, they serve two purposes: a) information can be read; b) information can be edited/updated by the people as well giving rise to the community involvement. Using wikis – web pages for the libraries can be created collaboratively and speed up the updating process (web pages) among the libraries. One of the nicest features the most wikis give, they allow one to see the page history meaning that users are able to recognize what has been edited/updated to a particular page and in such cases they provide a mechanism to the changes and compares the previous and current page versions.

RSS IN LIBRARIES

"RSS (originally RDF Site Summary; later, two competing approaches emerged, which used the backronyms Rich Site Summary and Really Simple Syndication respectively) is a type of web feed which allows users and applications to access updates to websites in a standardized, computer-readable format. These feeds can, for example, allow a user to keep track of many different websites in a single news aggregator" (Wikipedia,2019). It is an XML-based metadata content. The content on web if created or published at a certain place will be automatically received by the users who has subscribed to the feed. "RSS stands for Rich Site Summary or Really Simple Syndication. Syndication is a process that makes content on one website available to another website. It enables websites to share newly added content, major headlines and even summaries. The sharing of content usually takes place between a particular website and the website of an aggregator. This communication occurs in the form of basic XML that is both human and machine-readable" (geeksforgeeks.com).An XML-based (eXtensible Markup Language) format mainly used for the distribution of content Libraries are offering feeds of new materials, blog posts, and event information. Making use of RSS is one of the simplest and easiestway to remain up to date about the new events/ new information and so on in the library. Users don't need to click or check library website daily to see what is new. They can receive these notifications to their feeds directly. Library RSS may include the news about the library, latest information on a particular subject, and also may highlight the annual events of the library. RSS in the library can have multifold uses and can be used to provide bibliographic services, bulletin board services, Current Awareness Service and Selective Dissemination of Information and further can be used to marketize other library services as well.

SOCIAL NETWORKING SITES AND LIBRARIES

Social networking technologies provide large opportunity to the users to interact, create and share content. Social Networking Sites (SNS) have created a huge buzz in the last decade and they have billions of users all across the globe. Sites such as Facebook, YouTube, Twitter, Instagram, LinkedIn, WeChat and others have taken the world population by surprise given their use by the people of all ages. These sites can be used to create conversations, establish relationships, and develop connection with the people having common interests. These sites allow users to leave comments, provide feedback. It is an undeniable reality that most of the world's population is connected to social networking sites. Social networking sites have millions of users in India as well belonging to different age groups. So, these sites cannot only be used to manage relationships across geographical lines, but can also be used for academic purposes. In the context of libraries, SNS are important facets which can be used for maximizing the usage of library resources and marketing of library. Notwithstanding with the geographical locations, the sites readily allow libraries to engage their users, inform and update them about the housed library resources.

CONCLUSION

Library 2.0 is a concept highly different from that of traditional library services which aims at fulfilling the needs and expectations of today's library users by making the information readily available to the user irrespective of location and time, and it also ensures that obstacles to the information access are removed and shackles are broken, and seeks to ensure that barriers to use and reuse the information are removed. It may be referred as a model for library service which encourages and enhances the continuous purposeful change in the services, functions of the library. Making use of technology to provide services and fulfill the missions of the library is the sole aim of the library. With the adoption of web 2.0, users who wish not to visit library can gain a lot by just visiting the library blog, page etc. With web 2.0, the library can enhance its functionality- getting proper and valuable feedback from the users about their services and so on. Web 2.0 will enable libraries to eliminate costs incurred on marketing or advertising.

REFERENCES

O'Reilly, T. 2005. What is Web 2.0, O'Reilly Network. Available at: http://www.oreilly.de/artikel/web20.html. Accessed 15 January 2020

Rosen, D., & Nelson, C. (2008).Web 2.0: A new generation of learners and education.*Computers in the Schools*, *25*(3-4), 211-225., DOI: *10.1080/07380560802370997*

Habib, M.C. (2006), Toward Academic Library 2.0: Development and Application of a Library 2.0 Methodology, School of Information and Library Science, University of North Carolina at Chapel Hill, NC, available at: http://etd.ils.unc.edu/dspace/handle/1901/356 (accessed 26 Jan 2020).

Casey, M. E., &Savastinuk, L. C. (2007). Library 2.0: a guide to participatory library service. Information Today, Inc.

Wallis, R. (2007). WEB 2.0 TO LIBRARY 2.0–FROM DEBATE TO REALITY: A presentation to the cpd25 Conference, 23 April 2007, London.*New Review of Information Networking, 13*(1), 53-64.

Stephens, M., & Collins, M. (2007).Web 2.0, Library 2.0, and the hyperlinked library.*Serials Review, 33,* 253–256. doi:10.1016/j.serrev.2007.08.002

Maness, J.M. (2006). Library 2.0 Theory: Web 2.0 and Its Implications for Libraries. *Webology, 3.*

https://www.forbes.com/sites/robertadams/2017/03/02/top-income-earning blogs/#2dd4d21f2377

https://www.geeksforgeeks.org/introduction-to-rssrich-summary-site/

http://www.ala.org/tools/atoz/library-20

4
Digital Library

MEANING OF DIGITAL LIBRARIES

The emergence and development of digital libraries have created the new ways to gain access to quality education, e-Learning and research and at the same time preserving the cultural heritage for the generations to come. The potential that these ICT based digital libraries offer has an unprecedented value to offer to the informal learners as well and have led to the creation of job opportunities to them as well. The developments in the technologies that have taken place in the last few decades have had an enormous effect on the functionality of every organisations/institution. As libraries store their data in the databases, so it becomes inevitable for them to use digital or electronic technology to fulfill their mission and objectives. It is possible only through these technologies that such huge chunk of data/information can be accessed easily with minimum hindrances. In the absence of technologies and web, it would have been very complex and hard to find the required information easily in the current digital era. Digital libraries have become the forefront that have dramatically provided a shift in how information services are being offered to the users. Modern time digital libraries are rich in content available in variety of formats and retrieval access to the content can be reached through simple search interfaces. The authors gave different names to the digital libraries "library without walls or walls free electronic stations". Digital Libraries are the ones that gives a user an easy experience to use, access, downloadand share the information. The process that takes place in these libraries involves: information is digitized in the first instance, followed by collection using computers and transmitted via computer networks and in the final stage it can be freely shared. Using computer networks facilitates the efficient use and retrieval of the information.

DEFINITIONS OF DIGITAL LIBRARY

In the age of information explosion much is talked about the concept of digital libraries. The main reason for establishing digital libraries (DLs) is that they will help and provide access to a good number of information sources. Information or any update posted in the website was available only to the professionals working in the library but now given the fact that excessive use of electronic gadgets and other devices by the people help them to retrieve the demanded information as per their preferences. Libraries over a very long period of time have continued to be the repositories of knowledge produced by humans. Both in the past and present as well, libraries are considered as one of the coreelements of any institution and amounts significantly towards the strengths of an institution (Koohang&Durante,2003). Cleverland (1998) puts definition of digital library as "libraries with same purposes, functions, and goals as traditional libraries-collection development and management, subject analysis, index creation, provision of access, reference work and preservation, A narrow focus on digital formats along hides the extensive behind the scenes work that libraries do to develop and organize collections and to help users find information". Education plays a pivotal and extraordinary role in the progress of the economy of any nation. India is a country where a number of students "left education" both primary and higher education due to some unavoidable circumstances like poverty, unavailability of resources and non-availability of seats (limited seats) in the higher educational institutions. To cater these obstacles that come in the way of getting education to the large masses, the open educational resources provided by the digital libraries can be a positive and giant step in that direction. The importance of digital libraries in such scenario proves to be the vital and which can render positive benefits. Digital libraries elsewhere across the globe are rapidly becoming the pivotal at higher educational institutes as they allow the access to their multiple contents on remote basis all days of the week to the infinite number of users, doing away with the physical visits, by combining technology and information services and resources and providing these resources in the form of videos, audios, texts and so on. Over the past decade many digital libraries were built across the globe and several initiatives were taken to enhance their capabilities (Coleman & Sumner, 2004). In supporting the teaching and learning process, NSDL, has been taking, on continuous basis, a multifold innovative services which include: "services supporting personalized content delivery, services for creating digital resources, and communication and collaboration services" (NSDL,2003).

So, it may be said that a digital library resembles an information system having variety of components that include human resources, collections, resources, a computer system and networking.

ADVANTAGES OF DIGITAL LIBRARIES

There are number of advantages digital libraries offer to the users, providing fast interrupt access both in campus and remote, ensuring the retrieval efficiency, helps in identifying the relevant sources and keeping the irrelevant out of search results, provides richer user interface and there is no bound or limit on the number of copies that a user can access, supports multimedia content, supports formal and informal learners, provides advanced search options, provides unique referencing for digital objects etc.

The main advantages are following:

Diverse Choice : Traditional libraries used to provide services to a limited clientele as well as access to limited library resources but in case digital libraries a user has a variety of choices beforehand i.e. a user can have access to multiple library resources against his/her demands.

Preservation of Culture and Heritage : Digital libraries not only provide access to information resources but also preserve the cultural values of the societies for the future generations. Fire, floods and other natural or man-made calamities proved disastrous to the resources available in the traditional libraries and resulted in the destruction of rich cultural heritage of many nations. In digital libraries the electronic copies of these can be replicated and protected from any damage.

Information/ Resources can be shared : One of the major benefits of DLs is networking i.e. hosting the content on the library website can be easily shared with anybody.

Quick access to the information resources : Rapid access to the information resources in the digital library makes it a unique choice for the all the users who always run of time and who don't wish to visit the library physically. The content in the digital libraries can be accessed anywhere, all one needs is proper internet connectivity.In simplest terms it may be said that with the digital library, information is brought to user's desk 24*7.

Currency of the Content : Currency and Updation of any website makes it top choice among the user communities. The website that hosts latest/ up to date information can have much visitors as compared to ones which is least updated.

Easier information retrieval : To retrieve or extract the information from the digital libraries a variety of searching techniques have been developed over the past few years which include truncation, proximity, boolean operators and so on. These operators help the users to gain efficiency in the retrieval process

Rich Interaction : Digital libraries provide a rich and effective access to the information stored on its databases and helps a user to search accordingly from the varied options available on the digital library website.

SERVICES PROVIDED BY DIGITAL LIBRARIES

The services of digital libraries vary a lot from those of traditional based library systems where every activity was carried out involving the use of paper or printed materials but in case of digital library, providing user the library services mainly takes place in an online environment. Here are the few services that digital libraries provide: E-book service, access to journals provided online both on campus and off campus users, email services, Current awareness services, selective dissemination of information service, and alerts to the users about the new arrivals, CD Rom services, access and links to union catalogues etc.

NEED AND CHALLENGES OF DIGITAL LIBRARIES

Every minute billions of bytes of information is created that leads to the creation of information explosion, so the concept of a system comes into effect that can handle and manage the information explosion. With the presence of digital libraries, access to high quality content and research can be easily provided to the users and put the "garbage information" (unwanted information/ results) at bay. Secondly, traditional libraries lack of space as collections build every year, so in order to solve the space problems and its related costs, DLs seem to be the best alternative. To build a DL, following methods are followed: Digital Media Acquisition, content creation, DL website/ Portal, converting the old contents to digital forms etc.

One the one hand, digital libraries seem to solve the space and information retrieval problems but on the other hand they come with certain challenges. The major challenges that DLs face is that their establishment wholly and revolves rounds the facets of technology as their creation, document uploading, collection building, and disseminating the same relies heavily on technology. Librarians these days have the acute shortage of funds and resources and they problems they face be the reluctance of library staff to work in a digital environment or lack of motivation may be the reasons behind that. Continuous updating of the library database / website also poses big challenge libraries face in the digital environment

DIGITAL LIBRARIES AND ROLE OF STAFF

The arrival of "digital age" has brought a remarkable shift and changes in how information /knowledge is created, stored, organised, acceded and disseminated. With this complete shift from traditional to modern libraries, the meaning and concept of Librarian has also changed. Often, the staff working in the libraries in this era are labeled as information professionals. For effective management and functioning of the digital libraries, the library staff must possess the required competencies for the smooth working of a library. The way and the pace at which information is being created with the help of technological tools enforces librarians to change their traditional practices and approaches. The main access points in the libraries- catalogues used to be in the print form in traditional libraries. Now a days in digital or virtual libraries the access points are highly customized and computerized and facilitate an easy access to the library resources. This means to provide or facilitate access to the library resources; the staff needs to be experts and highly trained (technically) in the library so that resources delivery is done in the best way.

The competencies needed for managing digital collection relates to different environment. In such cases, librarian, in addition to act as library manager, also becomes as collection development, technical processor, reference librarian, taking care of information quality. In such scenario the role of the staff in the library changes, as librarians role, to run the library becomes that of "information manager" who has to manage the information and meet the required needs of the diverse population. In addition, the human resources in such cases should be able to design, network and develop an efficient and effective information system. The people assigned to work in a digital environment should possess Knowledge management skill, Information Technological skill (i.e. design applications, archiving of knowledge, systems, websites etc.), leadership skills involving communication and strategic management and professional marketing skills to boost the services of the library. In the technological era much preference is given to the libraries that use sophisticated technology and digital libraries seems to be doing the same. In the future, digital libraries need to put together resources, ICT tools that may prove beneficial in dissemination of library information and reference services and this can only be done by the libraries having skilled staff who are well experienced in handling the technology. The librarians in the modern era have to work differently, much differently than they used to be working during the traditional ones. They have to equip and adapt themselves with the latest technology

GENERAL OVERLOOK OF SOME NATIONAL DIGITAL LIBRARIES

National Digital Library of India

In India the National Digital Library of India (NDL India) is a pilot project developed by Indian Institute of Technology Kharagpur under the aegis of Ministry of Human Resource Development (MHRD). The main aim of this digital initiative in India is "to provide support for all academic levels including researchers and life-long learners, all disciplines, all popular form of access devices and differently-abled learners". As on 10 September, 2020 NDL India hosts 50,255,112resources in its database. NDL India holds various types of resources both in born digital and in converted form. The resources include audio-visual materials, books, thesis and other content which are of great educational value which can be used by anyone both formal and non-formal learners and access to the library is without any charge. The library website can be accessed in 8 Indian languages including English.

Searching Facility : The resources available at the NDL can be accessed by with a single-window search facility. Also to save the time and effort and to provide efficiency in the retrieval process a Filtered and federated searching can applied .

Availability of Content : The NDLI holds the educational contents from primary to PG level and are available in 70 different languages and the repository holds more than 60 types of learning resources including the fields of Technology, Science, and Humanities etc.

Books and Articles : The library contains a rich repository of more than seven lakh books available in 70 different languages and over three lakh articles by different publishers.

Audio/Video Lectures : NDL India contains a very rich number of audio and video lectures on different subjects. More than 262 and a booming and ever increasing 18000 plus video lectures can be watched on the library's website.

Featured Sources : The featured sources available on the NDL are: NPTEL, NCERT, ShodhGanga and LibriVOx which holds more than 2 lakh audio books.

Screengrab of NDL India showing the "Leraning Resource Type" content.

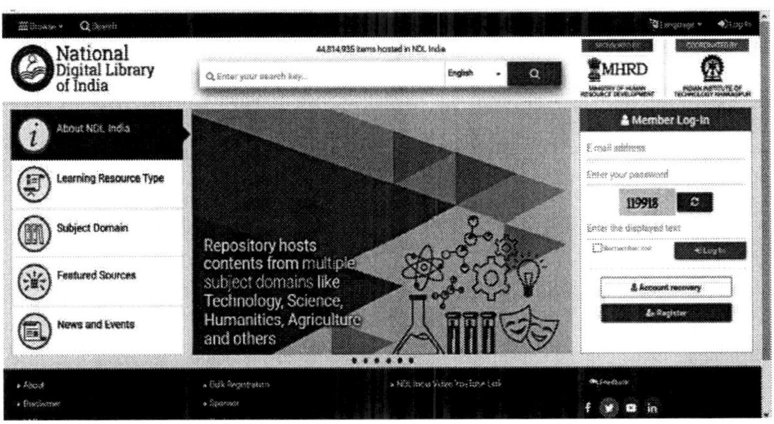

Image depicts that NDL India hosts content for different subject doamains.

Image showing content is available in 70 languages. (NDL India)

National Digital Library of China

The concept and the development of digital library started in China started in mid-1990s when the ICT has a giant effect on the lives of people as to how they share, communicate and save the information. In early 2000, projects of national level in the development of digital libraries were undertaken by "National Library of China, National Technology and Science Library, China Academic Library and Information System, National Science Library" which ensured the developing phase of establishing DL in the country. It was in late 90's when the National Library of China worked on developing the DL in the country and its efforts proved beneficial as the project was completed. "The goal of the project was to establish a digital library service that provides all the functionality of the Chinese National Library, and implements mechanisms and procedures for collection, digitization, and archiving of Chinese information resources, accumulates a very large amount of high quality digital resources, provides access to those resources over the Internet, establishes a platform for technical support of digital resource collection, enhancement, storage and management, provides a digitized Chinese information service in China and around the world via the Internet, establishes the largest and most complete digital Chinese information collection and provides services for it, and makes it part of the foundation of the national information service" (Zhen,2010).

SEARCHING FEATURES IN NDLC

The searching features that are available at the NDLC website and users can extract resources are: Wenjin Search, OPAC, Featured Resources, Resources from Local Libraries and Site Search.

Books and Dissertations

The library also provides access to books both Chinese and Foreign and access to dissertations both local include "China Doctoral/Master Dissertation Database (CNKI), China Proceedings of Conference Full-text Database (CNKI), Full-text Database of Academic Conferences in China (Chinese version), Full-text Database of Academic Conferences in China (English version), NLC Digitalized Doctoral Dissertations and Post-doctoral Research Report Database and in foreign category the list includes ProQuest Dissertations & Theses: Foreign Language Dissertations Full-text Database , ProQuest Dissertations & Theses: A & I, EEE/IEE Electronic Library (IEL)".

Audio/Video Databases

The library provides access to "Suridea Learning" a platform that covers BBC, CNN and VOA and covers variety of columns series on New Technology, Jobs and Health. The programmes levels are divided according to the understanding level of the users and the level is divided into three sections advanced, intermediate, and primary.

TOFO Audible Digital Library : This section is dedicated to Chinese and foreign classics, humanities, social sciences and household encyclopedias. The contents can be used in audible and readable form.

Audio-visual Digital Resources Database : This contains the audio and video lectures on education and politics, economy and industry culture, agriculture, and medicine. The facility by the users can be availed in reading room or through the VOD system on the LAN.

YALE Classic Cinema Database : The databases serves users on the demand basis providing videos, TV series, films that are produced and made in the Chinese mainland, Hong Kong, Taiwan, Japan, South Korea, Europe, and America.

Video Library : This platform deals and provides information on foreign education, science and teaching programs in English medium with Chinese subtitles.

DIGITAL PUBLIC LIBRARY OF AMERICA (DPLA)

"The Digital Public Library of America empowers people to learn, grow, and contribute to a diverse and better-functioning society. We do this by maximizing public access to our shared history, culture, and knowledge. DPLA connects people to the riches held within America's libraries, archives, museums, and other cultural heritage institutions. All of the materials found through DPLA—photographs, books, maps, news footage, oral histories, personal letters, museum objects, artwork, government documents, and so much more—are free and immediately available in digital format. The cultural institutions participating in DPLA represent the richness and diversity of America itself, from the smallest local history museum to our nation's largest cultural institutions" (DPLA Website, 2020).

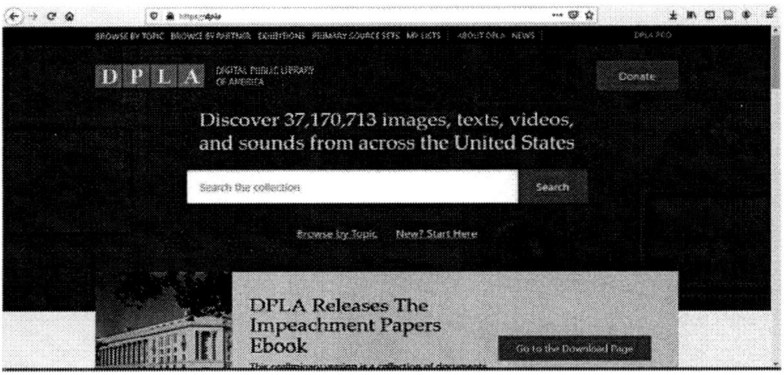

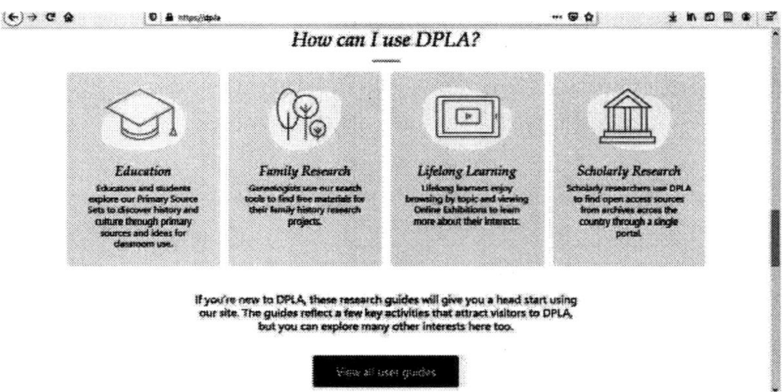

WORLD DIGITAL LIBRARY

"World Digital Library (WDL) is a project of the U.S. Library of Congress, carried out with the support of the United Nations Educational, Cultural and Scientific Organization (UNESCO), and in cooperation with libraries, archives, museums, educational institutions, and international organizations from around the world. The

WDL makes available on the Internet, free of charge and in multilingual format, significant primary materials from all countries and cultures. The principal objectives of the WDL are to: a) Promote international and intercultural understanding; b) Expand the volume and variety of cultural content on the Internet; c) Provide resources for educators, scholars, and general audiences; d) Build capacity in partner institutions to narrow the digital divide within and between countries".

DIGITAL LIBRARIES AND E-LEARNING

At a time when the most of the educational and scholarly resources are under commercial pay walls, the role of digital libraries in a developing country like India in providing access to the resources to formal and non-formal learners becomes highly important. In most of the cases, the e-Learning takes place on all days of week and access to the resources can be provided to any user in the country. India as it stands the second most populous country in the world and is the home to one of the highest number of higher education students is grappling with certain problems in providing quality education and equal access to the educational masses.

Other prominent digital libraries are :

Google books

Hathi trust Digital Library

Project Gutenberg

Internet archive contains e-books and audio books a non- profit library of movies, musicandwebsites.

CONCLUSION

In the digital environments the main aim of the digital libraries remains to provide timely and efficient access to the users based on their demands regardless of the boundaries. This is possible only when the operators of such libraries are laced with the competent human resource and adequate infrastructure. Digital libraries in the academic institutions are more focused on the academic subjects taught in the respective institutions. Digital libraries save the time of users and provide them better results. The coming of information technology has led to a shift from industrial to information society. In the current scenario, information and communication technologies are used for creating, organizing, storing and disseminating the information. Adoptionof ICT tools in the libraries have changed the concept of libraries when compared to their past settings. DL facilitates wide range of services and functions to the resources which were absent in the traditional libraries. Resources can be accessed all days of the week at any time at faster speeds. Also, the preservation of content can be ensured for the longer periods and the theft/ damage or misuse of library resources can be eliminated to the greater extents. Digital libraries have a double role to play i) providing access to quality materials in the information explosion era; ii) preservation of national heritages. Conversion of archives into digital objects and other library resources have witnessed an upward trend in the last few decades all because of the digitization process. Moreover, they are aimed to be built for providing intellectual access to the resources housed in the libraries. Using the modern technology, national digital libraries and repositories are built. Digital Libraries particularly in China and India have a major and substantial role to play in providing the equitable access to the quality resources. As the technology is evolving and developing on the regular basis, the digital libraries need to keep pace with it in implementing the latest technological advancements as to reap the maximum benefits to the societies and can heavily transform the learning process.

REFERENCES

NSDL (2003) National Science Digital Library Progress Report, Fall

2000 - Summer 2003, p. 29 *http://nsdloutreach.comm.nsdl.org/annual_report/2003/NSDL.Rpt.final.Pgs_25-32.pdf*

Zhen, X. (2010).Overview of digital library development in China.*D-Lib Magazine, 16*(5), 1.

Koohang, A., & Durante, A. (2003).Learners' perceptions toward the web-based distance learning activities/assignments portion of an undergraduate hybrid instructional model.*Journal of Informational Technology Education, 2*, 105–113.

Cleveland, G. (1998), "Digital libraries: definitions, issues, and challenges", available at: *www.ifla.org//VI/5/op/udtop8/udt op8.pdf.*

Coleman, A., & Sumner, T. (2004). Digital libraries and user needs: negotiating the future. *Journal of Digital Information, 5*(3).

DPLA Website (2020). Retrieved at : https://dp.la/about

5

Information Literacy, Digital Information Literacy, Media and information Literacy in Indian Perspective

INTRODUCTION

We are living on super-actively burning volcano of information where in every single minute billions and millions of information are bombarding. This is happening because we are in such a horizon where everything is in our palm and just a click away. From early morning to late night, spontaneously, we are reliant on computers and social media. These are connected with high-speed internet connectivity and believed to be one of the significant information producers. One can imagine that how much information are created and available to us with this few examples; on Google search engine, when we googled with several keywords such as 'information' about 25,27,00,00,000 results within (0.46 seconds) appeared with the keyword 'economy' about 3,18,00,00,000 results within (0.47 seconds) and with 'technology' about 17,76,00,00,000 results (0.48 seconds) retrieved to us. From this very minor example it is clear that, information is likely to be uncountable and enormous in numbers. A report by Subin (2019) showed, how first information is growing unprecedentedly in the quantum of information, that in every 60 seconds, 18.1 million text messages are sent, 3.8 million search queries on google (only one search engine), 2.1 million chats are created on Snapchat, 41.6 million messages are sent on WhatsApp and Messenger, 188 million emails are sent, 87,500 peoples are twitting, 4.5 million videos are viewed on YouTube, 1 million logging in Facebook etc. Though it is not a clear picture of entire ocean of information from where information is created. Now if we are trying to get idea pertaining to printed information, the report of STM mentioned that more than 3 million articles are published by scholarly peer reviewed journals throughout the countries. One cannot easily guess what may be the total number of articles if non-peer reviewed articles are included with peer reviewed. Eventually,the invention of printing press by Guttenberg in the year 1439, welcomes a revolution in publication arena. However, it is also a fact that all information is not useful and reliable. Some of them are irrelevant, some are unreliable and junk, even some are fake. Therefore, it is a difficult job to identify the reliable, useful and authentic information. Because of these above mentioned reasons, the notion of 'information literacy' and 'information competency' 'digital information literacy, and 'media literacy' came in the realm.

BACKGROUND OF INFORMATION LITERACY

The connotation 'information literacy' is not a new concept at all, although, it has become popular in 2010s with emerging of 'information society'. Subsequently, the term 'information literacy' as it is now, cannot be marked to any single author or researcher's work/study. In fact, it is also difficult to find out any single reason or driving force in its existence. By the way, it is noticed that nearly 50 years back, in the year 1974, a paper prepared by, Paul Zurkowski, then president of 'Information Industry Association, USA, mentioned the term "information literate" by this he meant people, who were to survive in the race of emerging information society (Horton, 2008). In that time, it was established as a necessity to compete with information overload. So that, a person can easily articulate his information requirement to solve his/her problem and make decision at own level (Horton & UNESCO, 2014) but nevertheless, it is equally relevant at present juncture. Since, then the concept is playing on the playground of information competency, information society, and information skill etc.

WHAT IS INFORMATION LITERACY?

The concept of information literacy has gained its momentum due to exponential growth of e-resources, different databases, particularly, due to shifting user behavior in relation to searching information for self-learning, doing research and for various individual or social work (Umesh, 2018).Information literacy is a typical pedagogy based some learning instruction in schools, colleges, universities and libraries, intends to make the users capable to solve their problems by their own. Information literacy is a process where one shall be competent enough to identify his/her required information, places where it may locate, way to get that information, evaluation of information in the perspective of accuracy, authenticity, reliability and make best use of it judiciously to quench his/her information thirst in day-out and day in (Chen & Lin, 2011). Like learning, it is a lifelong process which may take place at any stage of our life from childhood to old age (Yýlmaz & Soylu, 2014). Because, we do work at different time and different level and for that work information is required, no matter, whether information is availing through formal or informal channels. Information literacy is reflected as prerequisite for a user (students, faculty, researchers, scientists etc.) to access and contentious use of information from various formats (print and electronic) in order to be self-empowered. Information literacy is bicentric mechanism where 'user' is one side while 'use of information' on the other side.

DEFINITIONS OF INFORMATION LITERACY

There are dozens of definitions given by different organizations and persons all over the world, as far as information literacy is concerned, UNESCO, SCONUL, CILIP and ALA are prominent of them.

According to UNESCO (2005) "*Information literacy empower people in all walks of life to seek, evaluate, use and create information effectively to achieve their personal, social, occupational and educational goals*".

As Johnston & Webber (2003) defines "*Information literacy is the adoption of appropriate information behaviour to identify, through whatever channel or medium, information well fitted to information needs, leading to wise and ethical use of information in society.*" P. 336

The most widely cited definition given by ALA (1989) "*To be information literate, a person must be able to recognize when information is needed and have the ability to locate, evaluate and use effectively the needed information*" (p. 1)

The pioneer organization in the context of giving information literacy model, SCONUL, Bent & Stubbings (2011) in the paper 'The SCONUL Seven Pillars of Information Literacy: Core model' defines it as "*Information literate people will demonstrate an awareness of how they gather, use, manage, synthesize and create information and data in an ethical manner and will have the information skills to do so effectively.*" (p.1)

SIGNIFICANCE OF INFORMATION LITERACY

The notion 'information literacy' is an inseparable component of 'Information for All', a UNESCO program, considered as a basic right to human beings (UNESCO, 2005). In addition to it, once Mr. Obama, the then president of USA, emphasized information literacy as a novel kind of literacy requisite to the 'functioning of our modern democratic society' and essential for effective and efficient navigating the 'information age' in which we live in (Demasson et al., 2019).

In present scenario, internet is like oxygen. In the context of Information and Communication Technology (ICT), internet and technology (tools, gadgets) both are equally important. All these together, keep producing abundant information. In addition to it, information is blood, without it we cannot think of anything. Therefore, there is a tremendous need of information literacy to make fulfill our information demand with proper understanding at our own ability. It will help to develop a skill to handle enormous and complex variety of information. Here, some points are given below;

1. Lifelong Learner : Information literacy will make the tendency of learning through the life for better quality of decision making at different stage of life. There is no end of learning; more and more learning will make a person wiser and better decision maker (Demasson et al., 2019).

2. Information Competency : By information literacy, a person will be able to judge the quality, reliability and value of information which is verily essential due to the rolling up of fake news.

3. Critical Thinking : It will also help to create the capability of critical thinking, what is the problem, what is the solution of that problem, how to solve that problem and so on. In another way, it may say that it will help in problem based learning process (Chen & Lin, 2011).

4. Information Ethics : Another worth mentioning objective of information literacy is making a person aware about different kinds of rights, such as; copyright, intellectual property right.

ROLE OF LIBRARIES IN INFORMATION LITERACY

As far as libraries are concerned 'imparting information, 'information dissemination' 'information competency skill' are some of the fundamental objectives. By saying 'libraries' it meant different types of libraries; School library, College and University Library and Public Library as well.

In the context of school library and information literacy, as (Knezevic, 2013) pointed "*it is in this form of literacy education school library should have an important role because it teaches students self-design - research, encourages them to creative and critical thinking in finding, selecting, evaluating and applying information*" (p.63). If children are flower then schools are garden where flowers (children) bloom, and the school libraries can play a very significant role to bloom this flower in a well nurtured way. In true sense, at schools children become familiar with the bookish world and other documents. Therefore, libraries right from the beginning can make curious and enthusiastic reader who will feel excitement of reading and writing. Simultaneously, library will make the children familiar with authentic sources of reliable information, importance of authentic information, location where it may be available. These things are the initial stages of information literacy which will make children self-empowered to solve their problem with their own competency. In this regard, librarians should encourage, motivate them to use library at their best level and inculcate reading habit, importance of literacy and competency, how to utilize the gadgets in rational way and create the habit of library use (Knezevic, 2013).

As it is well known that 'libraries are the heart of

universities' (higher education system).The role of library and librarians are no more to just as custody and custodian of information rather it should be a place of learning. Librarian should be imparting knowledge to its users and make them learned, competent, empowered, and information literate in order to help the users floating and navigating on information ocean (Chen & Lin, 2011). It is pertinent to mention here in the context of college and university libraries and information literacy, Association of College and Research Libraries (ACRL) (2000) described some basic competencies as; *"identify a variety of types and formats of potential sources for information", "select the most appropriate investigative methods or information retrieval systems", "determine whether the new knowledge has an impact on the individual's value system and takes steps to reconcile differences"* (p. 7-12). From the above competencies, it is understood that libraries/librarians should offer library orientation programs, user orientation programs, workshops on different databases and information retrieval, copy right, plagiarism and intellectual property rights, and also how to deal unauthentic and junk information. Librarians, also, should make the users aware about ILL, DDS and SDI services which will help to get information from other network libraries in case of unavailability of those in their own library. Hence, the librarian will make the students/users abled to search and retrieve their needed information with multiple strategies, asses the fetched results and obviously be able to make best use of it keeping in mind information ethics (Cordell, 2013).

The character of public libraries in mounting information literacy among the community is very much important and vast. Public library has a great responsibility in developing literacy among the community by providing different services as it is 'People's University'. As (Cordell, 2013)pointed out that information literacy is an integrated motive of public libraries. When a librarian assists a user, in getting accurate information on any particular event, item and anything is stepping ahead toward developing information literacy among them. Since, the public libraries are the hub of public for the purpose of reading, discussion, getting information, doing scholarly work etc., librarians can orient them how to search information from a source (database, journal, magazine, book shelves), how to use library web page, how to get one's desired information through smartphone, personal computer, laptop sitting at home.

INFORMATION LITERACY INITIATIVES IN INDIA

In Indian education system, information literacy initiatives have been taking place since long time in different forms and names, for instances; library orientation program, library visit, user education, workshop on library services, database workshop, research ethics workshop etc. by either universities, libraries, colleges, University Grant Commission or some other govt. and non-govt. institutions. However, the initiatives taken by Government of India are bit different, for example; District Primary Education Programme (DPEP), Sarva Shiksha Abhiyan (SSA), Rashtriya Madhyamik Shiksha Abhiyan (RMSA), National Literacy Mission (NLM), Saakshar Bharat, E-Pathshala, National Digital literacy Mission (NDLM), National Knowledge Commission (NKC), TARA Akshar, CBFL 'Computer-Based Functional Literacy', SWAYAM and so on in order to enhance the literacy rate and develop skill of self-learning and empowerment among the citizen of India.

MODELS OF INFORMATION LITERACY

There are plenty of information literacy models available by now, but the undoubtedly, most widely accepted one is 'Seven Pillars of Information Skills Model' given by "*The Society of College, National and University*

Libraries"(SCONUL). In the year 1999, SCONUL working group published a paper on information Literacy under the title "Information Skills in Higher Education: a SCONUL Position Paper" on which for the first time this popular model introduced. Since then, despite of appearing many related models by others, its adoptability and acceptability is incessantly increasing worldwide among the librarians, faculties and learned groups as a means of enabling themselves to imparting information literacy to their users or students (Bent & Stubbings, 2011). Even today, twenty years since it was introduced, it is relevant as it was at that time.

The model consists of seven competencies or skills named as pillar as; Identify, Scope, Plan, Gather, Evaluate, Manage, and Present. It is circular model, starts with identifying of problem (information need) and ends with presenting (use of information to accomplish one's need) and all the competencies are often closely connected each other. More than this, under each skill there is a 'set of attributes/ understanding'. Once a person builds understanding of literacy at own level, will be able to do certain jobs associated with it. The person who has more understandings and ability of action are having hierarchy in rank/position at the upper level of the pillar of this model

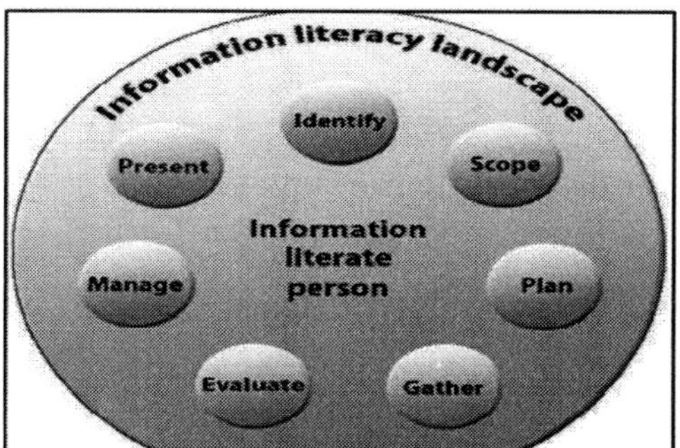

Fig. : Seven Pillar of Information Literacy Model by SCONUL Bent & Stubbings (2011)

Here, with each and every competency/skill and their associated understandings and ability of actions are discussed below;

Pillar-1: Identify (develop the ability/competency of identifying require information first)

Understandings

- Information is produced abundantly at every single moment therefore, motive to learn more and more and understands it as lifelong process.
- One has to inculcate learning habit to become aware about the new information.
- Subsequently, one should understand that information helps to develop some ideas or to enhance already existing knowledge.
- One should understand the published as well as unpublished data and information.

Ability

- One should be able to identify the gap (problem) in a particular domain.
- Ability to formulate question/problem and to present it easily.
- Ability to hold recent knowledge on that problem
- Ability to create zeal to have information in order to solve a problem.
- Ability to use prior knowledge to underpin the search
- Ability to search/acquire information independently

Pillar-2 : SCOPE (Judging the present information and finding out the gaps)

Understanding

- Understand the information and knowledge which are available at present.
- Understand the features of various information sources and they are changed in nature with the format such as print and electronic format.

- Understand the process of information publication in different forms and 'information as economy'.
- Understand the difficulties in accessing needed information
- Understand the services, available to get access of information.

Ability

- Ability to "know what you don't know" in order to point out the gaps.
- Ability to decide that what kind information is more suitable to meet the requirement
- Ability to have knowledge pertaining to the different types of information formats
- Ability to incorporate new tools for better use as when they become available

Pillar-3 : PLAN (developing a plan for getting needed information)

Understandings

- Understand the meaning and utility of search strategies for discovering information.
- Understand the differences between the available search tools
- Understand the benefits and drawbacks of search tools
- Understand the necessity to have different approaches for searching information with search tools
- Understand the necessity to change the 'search keyword' according to the nature of results
- Understand the significance of "controlled vocabularies" search strings and "taxonomies"

Ability

- Ability to recognize the most appropriate tools for searching needed information

- Ability to use most relevant keywords
- Ability to select most suitable techniques

Pillar-4 : GATHER (locating the place where needed information may be available)

Understandings

- Understand how information and knowledge is organised and repackaged
- Understand the library services to get access to information and knowledge
- Understand the difficulties in accessing new information
- Understand the use of abstract as well as indexing sources
- Understand the meaning and necessity of citation and references
- Understand the difference between open access and subscribes resources
- Understand the risk of virtual world

Ability

- Ability to keep up to date
- Ability to use complex, advance and federated search techniques
- Ability get full text information
- Ability to use different types of services offered by the libraries to get access to resources

Pillar-5 : EVALUATE (assessing the gathered information)

Understandings

- Understand how to assess the information
- Understand the quality, reliability, accuracy and relevance of information
- Understand the significance of uniformity in collecting information

- Understand the importance of proper citation/ references
- Understand how to publish information

Ability

- Ability to differentiate clearly available information sources
- Ability to select better search techniques for searching information and getting appropriate results
- Ability to justify the quality, reliability and credibility of gathered information
- Ability to critically analyze and making notes
- Ability to follow proper citation and references

Pillar-6 : MANAGE (organizing information professionally)

Understandings

- Understand the all the ethical aspects (copyright, plagiarism and intellectual property right) in handling information
- Understand the importance of systematic arrangements of information
- Understand the need to use and share information ethically
- Understand the role and importance of professionals and experts (librarians, information scientists and data managers) in information management

Ability

- Ability to use technology (softwares) for proper management of citation, reference and plagiarism)
- Ability to use different data management softwares effectively and efficiently for data management
- Ability to follow the standards for academic integrity

Pillar-7 : PRESENT (presenting the final results (new knowledge) in a attractive way by analyzing, synthesizing new and old information)

Understandings

- Understand the different ways of writing, presenting information to make it attractive to the communities
- Understand the self-responsibility in dissemination of information to the different community
- Understand the procedure of publication

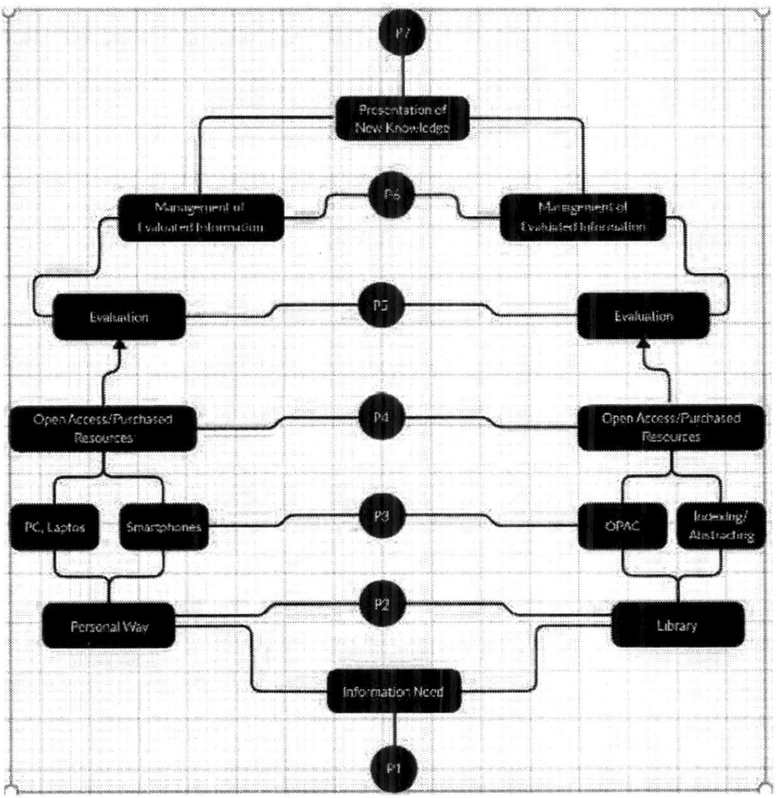

Fig. : Conceptual Framework of Information Literacy. (P = Pillar)

- Understand the use of technology (social media, ICT) to disseminate information

Ability

- Ability to make report, summary of gathered and analyzed information
- Ability to present the new information and knowledge among the different community effectively
- Ability to identify the appropriate outlets for publication and dissemination of new information
- Ability to use of technology by creating personal profile (ICT and SNS) judiciously for the dissemination of new information

DIGITAL INFORMATION LITERACY

The growth of digital information literacy is not as much faster as the changes of information communication technology is, and this imbalance creates an issue in higher education system Jeffrey et al. (2011). Paul Gilster has been credited for introducing the concept 'Digital Literacy, in 1997, as an extension to earlier term 'information literacy' where he claimed it as "mastering ideas, not keystrokes" (Nicholson, 2017). Digital literacy is all about the understanding of how do the technologies function and how to use these in a most appropriate manner to accomplish a work in a better way (Rantala, 2010). Usually, it is conceived as a multidimensional concept (Weber et al., 2018).

Digital Information Literacy (DIL) is a cluster of many 'life skills' and used as a synonym of 'Computer Literacy', 'Information Communication Technology Literacy', and 'Technological Literacy' although, these terms neither exact synonym of digital literacy nor giving the same meaning. But, these are used interchangeably or substitute of digital literacy (UNESCO, 2011). Digital information literacy is a multi-faceted connotation which connected with strategies for self-learning through lifelong way Jeffrey et al. (2011).

DEFINITION OF DIGITAL INFORMATION LITERACY

The term digital literacy has been described by (UNESCO, 2011)as *"...which include the use and production of digital media, information processing and retrieval, participation in social networks for creation and sharing of knowledge, and a wide range of professional computing skills"*.

According to Bawden (2001), digital information literacy is *"a set of attitudes, understanding and skills to handle and communicate information and knowledge effectively, in a variety of media and formats"*

As Jeffrey et al. (2011) defined it as *"digital information literacy involves recognising the need for, and being able to access and evaluate electronic information. The digitally literate can confidently use, manage, create, quote, and share sources of digital information in an effective way that demonstrates an understanding and acknowledgement of the cultural, ethical, economic, legal, and social aspects of information"* (p.385).

Therefore, based on the above definitions what it

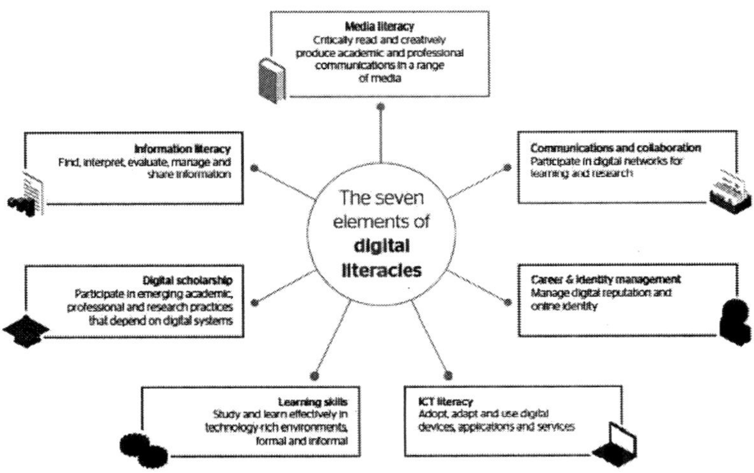

mean is digital information literacy means having all the pedagogical competencies of information literacy and in addition to it, having a sound skill of technology for the use of information/resources and of course, having a creative dimension in the outputs which will make an extra edge in the communication.

The seven elements of digital literacies given JISC

SKILLS OF DIGITAL INFORMATION LITERATE PERSON

Digital Literacy Task Force of American Library Association (2011) described the following skills of a digital literate person;

- Person must have the technical as well as cognitive skill of using technology for finding information, understanding the need, evaluate the information and to communicate information with ICT and other technologies in various formats.
- Person must be in a position to retrieve information, interpretation of information and assessing the quality of information with the appropriate use of technology.
- One should understand the relationship between technology, personal privacy, life-long learning and stewardship of information.
- Effective use of technology in the communication process with peers and public.
- One should know the proper use of technology in his/her own life-long learning and different activities of society.

DIGITAL INFORMATION LITERACY INITIATIVES BY GOVERNMENT OF INDIA

A mobile app namely Accessible India Campaign, Agrimarket App, BHIM (Bharat Interface for Money), Crime and Criminal Tracking Network & Systems (CCTNS), Crop Insurance Mobile App, Digital AIIMS, e-granthalaya, epanchayat, Ebiz, e-district, e-hospital, Epfo Web Portal & Mobile App, e-sampark, e-VISA, Farmer Portal, Geographic Information System (GIS), Knowledge Management System (KMS), m-Cessation, National Career Service Portal, National Knowledge Network, National Scholarship Portal (NSP), SWAYAM and Un-Reserved Ticket Through Mobile Application (UTS APP), Digital Disha Programme, MyGov.in, Unified Mobile Application for New-age Governance (UMANG), Digital Locker, e-Sampark(Digital India Programme, n.d.).

MEDIA AND INFORMATION LITERACY

Media Information Literacy is relatively new concept but highly popular not only among the scholars of media schools but it is also equally famous among the other scholars, educationists (Potter, 2010). UNESCO coined the umbrella term 'Media and Information Literacy' which connects 'media literacy' with 'information literacy' in order to emphasize the significance of scientific brainstorming capability for media and information users (Grizzle et al., 2011). Media and Information Literacy means a person should know the real use of information to fulfill his/her need ethically and, simultaneously, he/she should posses the skill of media use in all the pillars of information literacy for self-expression (Gretter & Yadav, 2016). Media and information literacy is the mingling of two ideas such as critical thinking ability and (Dezuanni, 2015). Here production means reproduction of information with the actual use of digital technology and media. The critical thinking skill purports the enhancement of one's ability to think scientifically and find out the solution of problem with information and knowledge.

DEFINITIONS OF MEDIA LITERACY

Siverblatt and Eliceiri (1997),in the Dictionary of Media Literacy, define the term media literacy as *"a critical-thinking skill that enables audiences to decipher the information that they receive through the channels of mass communications and empowers them to develop independent judgments about media content*" (p. 48).

Anderson (1981) defines it as the "*skillful collection, interpretation, testing and application of information regardless of medium or presentation for some purposeful action*" (p. 22).

Hence, media and information literacy can be summarized from the definitions as possessing the skill of functioning media and digital technologies in critical thinking, evaluation and reproduction as well as communication of information for better understanding and more impact among the users.

FIVE LAWS OF MEDIA LITERACY

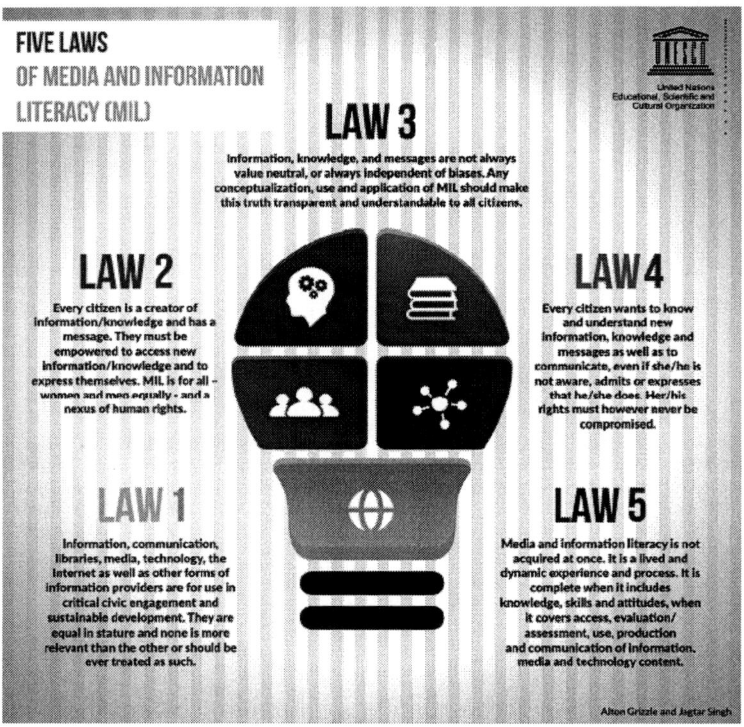

Singh et al. (2016)

SKILLS OF A MEDIA LITERATE PERSON

As Singh et al. (2016) defined the five competencies of a media and information literate person in UNESCO MILID yearbook as;

- Understanding the role and functions of media in democratic societies and development,
- Understanding the conditions under which media can fulfill its functions,
- Critically evaluating media content in the light of media functions,
- Engaging with media for self-expression and democratic participation, promoting intercultural and inter-religious dialogue, equality, peace, rights, countering hate and engaging in sustainable development;
- Reviewing skills (including ICTs) needed to produce user-generated content.

CONCLUSION

To deal with the huge and complex information in the present era, where information is produced and emerging tremendously, these literacies are very much required. Information Literacy, Digital information Literacy and Media Information Literacy are the widely discussed and core concepts in information society and knowledge society worldwide (Bawden, 2001). These three concepts directly or indirectly associated to fulfill the 4th and 16th Sustainable Development Goals of UNESCO that is 'Ensure Quality Education' and 'Peace and Inclusive Societies'. Subsequently, they are the important aspects of UNESCO's 'Knowledge Based Society' objective under the quadrants of; "Quality Education for all", Freedom of Expression", "Universal Access to Information" and "Multilingualism in Cyberspace" Singh et al. (2016). Therefore, in our educational system (primary, secondary, higher secondary or higher education), librarians and libraries should come forward to develop the enough competencies among the students to make them good decision maker, empowered, and life-long learner while in societies, it is the responsibility of the librarians of public libraries to build up the skills among the citizens to make them literate citizen and deal with complexity of information. These literacy skills will be essential and will be playing a significant role in the knowledge society as it is believed that information is continue to increase and the media use are also growing day by day.

REFERENCES

ALA. (1989). *Presidential Committee on Information Literacy: Final Report* [Text]. Association of College & Research Libraries (ACRL). http://www.ala.org/acrl/publications/whitepapers/presidential

ALA. (2011). *Digital Literacy, Libraries, and Public Policy* (pp. 1–27). https://districtdispatch.org/wp- content/uploads/2013/01/2012_OITP_digilitreport_1_22_13.pdf

Anderson, J. A. (1981). Receivership skills: An educational response. In M. Ploghoft & J. A. Anderson (Eds.), Education for the television age. Springfield, IL: Charles C. Thomas.

Association of College and Research Libraries (2000), "Information literacy competency standards for higher education", available at: www.ala.org/ala/mgrps/divs/acrl/standards/standards.pdf (accessed 02 Jan 2020)

B. S. (2019, December 28). This is What Happens in an Internet Minute. *Beebom.* https://beebom.com/what-happens-in-an-internet-minute-2019/

Bawden, D. (2001). Information and digital literacies: A review of concepts. *Journal of Documentation, 57*(2), 218–259. https://doi.org/10.1108/EUM0000000007083

Bent, M., & Stubbings, R. (2011). *The SCONUL Seven Pillars of Information Literacy: Core model.* SCONUL. https://www.sconul.ac.uk/sites/default/files/documents/coremodel.pdf

Chen, K., & Lin, P. (2011). Information literacy in university library user education. *Aslib Proceedings, 63*(4), 399–418. https://doi.org/10.1108/00012531111148967

Cordell, R., & Northern Illinois University. (2013). Information Literacy and Digital Literacy: Competing or Complementary? *Comminfolit,* *7*(2), 177. https://doi.org/10.15760/comminfolit.2013.7.2.150

Demasson, A., Partridge, H., & Bruce, C. (2019). How do public librarians constitute information literacy? *Journal of Librarianship and Information Science, 51*(2), 473–487. https://doi.org/10.1177/0961000617726126

Dezuanni, M. (2015). The building blocks of digital media literacy: Socio-material participation and the production of media knowledge. *Journal of Curriculum Studies, 47*(3), 416–439. https://doi.org/10.1080/00220272.2014.966152

Gretter, S., & Yadav, A. (2016). Computational Thinking and Media & Information Literacy: An Integrated Approach to Teaching Twenty-First Century Skills. *TechTrends, 60*(5), 510–516. https://doi.org/10.1007/s11528-016-0098-4

Grizzle, A., Wilson, C., & Unesco. (2011). *Media and information literacy curriculum for teachers.* United Nations Educational, Scientific and Cultural Organization. http://bibpurl.oclc.org/web/43202 http://www.unesco.org/new/fileadmin/MULTIMEDIA/HQ/CI/CI/pdf/publications/Media%20and%20information%20literacy%20curriculum%20for%20teachers.pdf

Horton, Forest W, & Unesco. (2014). *Overview of information literacy resources worldwide.* Unesco. http://infolit.org/wp-content/uploads/2014/10/UNESCO-IL-ResourcesEd.2.pdf

Horton, Forest Woody. (2008). *Understanding information literacy: A primer.* Unesco. https://unesdoc.unesco.org/ark:/48223/pf0000157020

Jeffrey, L., Hegarty, B., Kelly, O., Penman, M., Coburn, D., & McDonald, J. (2011). Developing Digital Information Literacy in Higher Education: Obstacles and Supports. *Journal of Information Technology Education: Research, 10,* 383–413. https://doi.org/10.28945/1532

Johnston, B., & Webber, S. (2003). Information Literacy in Higher Education: A review and case study. *Studies in Higher Education, 28*(3), 335–352. https://doi.org/10.1080/03075070309295

Knezevic, R. (2013). Information literacy and the role of the libraries in IT. *Romanian Journal of Library and Information Science, 9*(3), 63–66.

Nicholson, K. (2017). Objectives and actions. In *Innovation in Public Libraries* (pp. 127–135). Elsevier. https://doi.org/10.1016/B978-0-08-101276-5.00004-1

W. James Potter Ph.D. (2010) The State of Media Literacy. *Journal of Broadcasting & Electronic Media,* 54(4), 675-696, DOI: 10.1080/08838151.2011.521462

Rantala, L. (2010). Digital literacies as school practices. In *Practising Information Literacy* (pp. 121–141). Elsevier. https://doi.org/10.1016/B978-1-876938-79-6.50006-6

SERVICES | Digital India Programme. (n.d.). Retrieved January 6, 2020, from https://digitalindia.gov.in/rural

Silverblatt, A., & Eliceiri, E. M. E. (1997). Dictionary of media literacy. Westport, CT: Greenwood Press.

Singh, J., Kerr, P., & Hamburger, E. (2016). *Media and information literacy: Reinforcing human rights, countering radicalization and extremism; 2016.* Unesco.

UNESCO. (2005). *Information literacy | United Nations Educational, Scientific and Cultural Organization.* http://www.unesco.org/new/en/communication-and-information/access-to-knowledge/information-literacy/

UNESCO. (2011). *Digital literacy in education.* UNESCO IITE. https://iite.unesco.org/publications/3214688/

Weber, H., Hillmert, S., & Rott, K. J. (2018). Can digital information literacy among undergraduates be improved? Evidence from an experimental study. *Teaching in Higher Education, 23*(8), 909–926. https://doi.org/10.1080/13562517.2018.1449740

Yýlmaz, B., & Soylu, D. (2014). The Role of Public Libraries in Information Literacy in Turkey: A Study of a Provincial Public Library. In S. Kurbanoðlu, S. Špiranec, E. Grassian, D. Mizrachi, & R. Catts (Eds.), *Information Literacy. Lifelong Learning and Digital Citizenship in the 21st Century* (Vol. 492, pp. 642–651). Springer International Publishing. https://doi.org/10.1007/978-3-319-14136-7_67

6

Go for Green (G4G) : A Sustainable Development Approach in and of Library and Information Centres

INTRODUCTION

Due to several anthropogenic activities such as water, air, soil pollution, ozone layer depletion and increasing of greenhouse gases, our environment has become polluted. We are continuously pushing our beautiful living planet, The Earth; into a perilous situation (Kurbanoðlu & Boustany, 2014). Hence, global warming and climate change are now very alarming issues and burning topic for discussion everywhere around the world. Various activities, programs, initiatives are noticed at different places to make the masses aware about the effects and results of global warming and climate change at national, regional or international label. In this direction, United Nations held a talk where leaders from 193 different countries came together for discussion. As a result of it, "leaders from these countries created a plan called the Sustainable Development Goals (SDGs). This set of 17 goals imagines a future just 15 years off that would be rid of poverty and hunger, and safe from the worst effects of climate change" (United Nations Sustainable Development, n.d.). On the other side, since, libraries are the part of society and heart of educational institutions. As Aulisio beautifully said in his work that "Just because there might not be enough funds to build a new LEED certified building, and because librarians do not have the classroom time that instructors have, does not mean that the library cannot be a sustainability leader on campus" (Aulisio, 2013, 7).Therefore, libraries are also no more lagging behind from this global movement, Sustainable Development Goals (SDGs), to make our beautiful earth safe for living and passing it for future generations.

WHAT IS SUSTAINABLE DEVELOPMENT GOALS?

The Sustainable Development Goal is judicious use and conservation of natural resources (water, land, energy etc.) for upcoming generation(Kurbanoǒlu&Boustany, 2014).Sustainable Development Goals (SDGs) are a call for action by all countries irrespective of developed, developing or underdeveloped to foster prosperity by protecting our planet. The countries recognized that social issues such as poverty, health, social protection, education and so on can only be tackled by hand-in-hand with common strategies which leads toward economic growth and better society (United Nations Sustainable Development, n.d.). On 25th September 2015, United Nations (UN) in the presence of 193 leaders from all around the countries set ..." global goals to end poverty, protect the planet, and ensure prosperity for all as part of a new sustainable development agenda was adopted. Each goal has specific targets to be achieved over the next fifteen years" (Igbinovia, 2016). These seventeen goals are; "No Poverty; Zero Hunger; Good Health and Well-being; Quality Education; Gender Equality; Clean water and Sanitation; Affordable and Clean Energy; Decent Work and Economic Growth; Industry Innovation and Infrastructure; Reduced Inequalities; Sustainable Cities and Communities; Responsible Consumption and Production; Climate Action; Life below Water; Life on Land; Peace Justice and Strong Institutions; and Partnerships for the Goals" (United Nations Sustainable Development, n.d.).

Fig. : *Sustainable Development Goals* by (United Nations Sustainable Development, n.d.)

WHAT IS GREEN LIBRARY?

According to*Oxford English Dictionary* (1989) the term 'green' is "pertaining to, or supporting environmentalism" (p. 811). Generally, the metaphor "Green Libraries" are all about the overall green building movement.Green library is the combination of multi-facets and components, for instances green buildings, green activities and practices, green collection development and green information system and services (Kurbanoðlu & Boustany, 2014). The definition of green building as given by California Integrated Waste Management Board is "a structure that is designed, built, renovated, operated, or reused in an ecological and resourceefficient manner" (Green Building Basics, n.d.). In 2000, the United States Green Building Council set up and organization namely

LEED (Leadership in Energy and Environmental Design) which is a pioneer and leading body in gauging and certifying Green buildings (Antonelli, 2008; Brodie, 2012; Jankowska & Marcum, 2010; Woodland, 2010). As a result of library and Information Centers' involvement with environmental challenges, the "Green Library Movement" came out in the early 1990s, whose principal concern is to reduce the library and Information Centers' impact on environment, (Kurbanoðlu & Boustany, 2014). The phase 'Green Library' is library that is eco-friendly in nature from several ways and it follows the actions like; optimum utilization of electricity, using some sort of techniques and services which produce lesser carbon footprints in due process of information generation, organization, re-packaging, dissemination and publication (Antonelli, 2008; Jankowska & Marcum, 2010; Kurbanoðlu & Boustany, 2014). Online Dictionary of Library and Information Science (ODLIS) defines green libraries as: a building (library) which takes care of reducing the adverse effect on natural environment and trying to maximize the environmental quality of interior building by means of "careful site selection", "use of natural construction materials", "biodegradable products", and "conservation of resources" (responsible waste disposal, energy, water, recycling, and paper) during its build up (Malode, 2014; Thomas, 2017; Vijayalakshmi, 2018). Green library and its impact on SDGs is briefly defined by Aulisio as "I posit that a true green library is one that promotes sustainability by leading by example and attempts to incorporate sustainability into all aspects of academic librarianship. By engaging in these activities, librarians can support an ethical and academic mission of working within a sustainable lifestyle that will fully envelope their campus and beyond" (Aulisio, 2013, 1).

STRUCTURES OF GREEN LIBRARY IN THE CONTEXT OF SDGS

Building : According to Kurbanoðlu & Boustany (2014) green building is "a structure that is designed, built, renovated, operated, or reused in an ecological and resource efficient manner" (p. 50). Green buildings can help us to use our natural resources in a prudent manner and can optimize the carbon footprint rate. In order to build a building first we should take care in choosing a suitable place/site because the site has and great impacts on the SDGs. As Malode pointed out that library building should be in a densely populated and cluster areas which is surrounded with various service offices (Malode, 2014). The roof area of building should make in such a way so that it can drain rainwater into water storage tank which is then can be used for multi purposes such as water for irrigation of landscaped areas, toilet flushing, and other non-potable water uses(Brodie, 2012; Malode, 2014). Some of the salient features of green libraries as pointed out by Monika are "natural daylighting, shading to filter direct sunlight, solar panels, sensors that control indoor lighting for improved energy efficiency, and bamboo wood flooring... " (Antonelli, 2008, 4). In addition to this, "Sustainable aspects of library buildings include features such as lighting, ventilation, heating and cooling, the interior fittings, installing solar or geothermal energy systems, use of water-harvesting systems, double-paned windows, low-flush and dual-flush, all for electricity and water efficiency" (Kurbanoðlu & Boustany, 2014, 50).

Collection : As Kurbanoglu said "The problem of reducing a library's carbon footprints is perhaps the mostcomplex and most contentious when it comes to the format of the collection" (Kurbanoðlu & Boustany, 2014, 53). During the process of material selection, librarians' should keep it in their mind that only those materials which adopt green practices and produce less CO_2 should be given high importance over the noneco-friendly materials. Librarians should also exercise the recycling of the used paper or materials rather throwing it into open environment (Connell, 2010). In library, give more emphasize to electronic collection instead of print collection as Chowdhury discussed in his work that electronic version of materials are more sustainable instead. To mitigate the concern of responsible growth of space for shelves and power used, and Automated Storage Retrieval System (ASRS) can also be adopted (Brodie, 2012).

Operations and Practices : As far as library and information centers' operation and practices are concerned to achieve the sustainable development goals, they should incorporate but not limited to:

First of all, library should say 'No to Plastics or Eco-Foe Materials' and make judicious use of chlorine-free, FSC approved papers and they can separate the waste categorically and recycling the used materials and donating the weeding collection to the needy rather than using these to fill our land. Libraries can set their copier or printing machines 'default to duplex' and use both side instead of single side to reduce the environmental pressure. They should go with e communication and using eco-friendly cleaning products instead of toxic one. Libraries should make use of stairs instead of lift or escalators up to possible limits and make use of sensors for lights, water taps and wherever possible to reduce the energy consumption. Making sure that switch of all the electronic gadgets are off when its work is over. Increase the use of sunlight, ventilation and solar energy. All the electronic products those are in use inside library should be minimal energy consuming. Emphasizing on virtualization, so that multiple users can share a single machine's computing power. Try to repair the older gadgets/machines rather than purchasing new or disposing the older ones.Recycling,re-filling toner/ cartridges and choosing "green" inks (Kurbanoðlu & Boustany, 2014).

ROLE OF LIBRARIES IN ACHIEVING SUSTAINABLE DEVELOPMENT GOALS

Since, libraries are integrated part of our society and further public libraries are regarded as "People's University" and "Invisible College", it has a very vast role in regard of achieving SDGs by making people aware through various awareness drive, campaign etc. Hence, International Federation of Library Association and Institutions (IFLA) has come forward to lead the libraries all over the world, as torch bearer in this direction, to play a significant role in the society, from grass-root level to international level, in achieving SDGs of United Nations. Here the possible roles of libraries are given below;

Sl. No.	*SDGs*	*Role of Libraries*
1	No Poverty	Proper information/knowledge can help to increase the tangible or intangible assets available in a community. For instance, in a society where agriculture is the primary activities, if they get accurate information pertaining to the newly invention of pesticides, insecticides, what is the ideal ratio of land and fertilizer, what kind soil is suitable for which crops and so one. Then there is huge chance of increasing output which ultimately helps them to get more income. And as far as providing accurate information/knowledge on time is concerned, libraries are in the forefront to play this significant role in the society.
2	Zero Hunger	Poverty and hunger are inter-related to each other and directly proportionate as well. If poverty decreases then hunger will also decrease. Library can become a key player by making awareness about not to waste food, water and natural resources as well. Public libraries can also create food bank for the needy of the society to eradicate hunger. For example, in few places of West

		Bengal, India in collaboration of social workers, food banks are built up where they collect bread and curry from the willing civilians and distribute among the needy persons.
3.	Good Health & Well-being	All we know 'health is wealth'. In rural to extreme rural areas people are not aware about their own health. Libraries can make the people aware about their health information by driving health awareness programmes, medical consultancy programmes and also by arranging several sports competition. More importantly, library will make people aware about the bad effects of consumption nicotine, drugs and alcohol which are the major cause of health problem.
4.	Quality Education	It is one of the fundamental duties of libraries. It is very well-known to all of us that since centuries, many great philosophers, scientists achieved their knowledge from libraries rather going to any schools or institutions.
5.	Gender Equality	Libraries have to convey information and make civilians understood to through away their perception into the dustbin about gender inequality. At the same time, libraries have to come forward to make the female more literate and empowerment.
6.	Clean Water & Sanitation on	In the same way, libraries are supposed to aware the mass about the optimum use of resources, save water, harvesting rain water, use sanitations rather going to open. Libraries can give some awards yearly basis to best followers.
7.	Affordable & Clean Energy	One side library will use renewable energy, solar energy, using least energy consuming electronics, machines and gadgets, on the other side, library will create awareness among the society to do the same. Libraries also have to provide ICT services, proper light and electricity to ready, study rooms

		to the people for their development.
8.	Decent Work & Economic Growth	Libraries shall provide all the citizens irrespective of male or female, persons with differently abled equal facility for their employment and personality development through certain training, if it is required. For example, In European Union, each year 250,000 people get their jobs through their public libraries. This helps to go up their economic growth in both cases; domestic and national. Particularly, in developing and under developed countries it is highly necessary and important.
9.	Industry, Innovation & Infrastructure	Library and information centres should work as to access point of information technology, quality reading rooms, discussion rooms and endeavor to offer reasonably priced access to Internet facilities to those places where schools are little far. libraries should come ahead to make the students engaged in their reading, writing, lively debating, quizzes, and other learning activities so that they can use the modern development, sound infrastructure. So that students can use the libraries facility and in return they can give their best to the society.
10.	Reduce inequality	Library should encourage safe, dependable migration and also to follow the migration policy. Library should further extend their services, health, housing, education, residence, government benefits and legal supports to the new immigrants. In this paradigm, Toronto Public Library (Canada) is an example which facilitates all these services including 'Newcomer Settlement Services' to the immigrants.
11.	Sustainable Cities & Communities	Libraries should play a leading role to provide and protect any communities' or cities' invaluable cultural heritages and manuscripts for generations to come. It is one of the challenging responsibilities of the library to develop and exercise disaster and

	risk management center in collaboration with nations' disaster management center for protecting national precious resources from damage during any disaster.
12. Responsible Consumption	Libraries can encourage and advocate other organizations and institutions to adopt sustainable practices for the betterment of the world and environment.
13. Protect the Planet	Libraries play a major role in providing access to information and knowledge about climate change. They can also aware the mass about its dangerous effect on us.
14. Life below water	Libraries can hold their high image by providing information to sustainable use oceans, seas, and marine habitats in order to make a balanced environment for future. Library should also preserve the information of marine resources.
15. Life on Land	The landmass on which we residing in is becoming poisonous and unhealthy for us to live in, because of our continuous threats and misbehave with it. Therefore, libraries can contribute a lot to keep this land as suitable for habitant by educating people with different skills to save forest/greeneries, land in order to save our ecosystem.
16. Peace and Justice	Libraries should make internet access obtainable to the public at no or lower charge. Information centers can also provide guarantee of safeguard access to information as to defend necessary self-determinations, in accordance with national statute and international treaties
17. Partnership for the goal	As far as partnership for the goal is concerned, libraries or librarians irrespective of their types and size have a huge responsibility in developing inter-nations partnership by providing knowledge, path for collaboration.

STANDARDS OF GREEN LIBRARY/BUILDINGS

Leadership in Energy and Environmental Design

Leadership in Energy and Environmental Design (LEED) is the highest proclaimed certification program worldwide for standard of green building. It is initiated by the U.S. Green Building Council (USGBC), a non-profit organization. LEED certification standard has various ratings for the design, operation, construction and maintenance of commercial as well as domestic buildings separately. The rating levels are based on points; Certified (40-49 points), Silver (50-59 points), Gold (60-79 points), Platinum (80 and above).

Green Rating for Integrated Habitat Assessment

In India, Green Rating for Integrated Habitat Assessment (GRIHA) is a standard for the green building. It has guidelines for the development of green building with indigenous tools which will lead towards the environment friendly building. Here, GRIHA is developed by The Energy and Resources Institute, New Delhi (TERI).

Center of Science and Technology for Rural Development

Center of Science and Technology for Rural Development (COSTFORD) in Kerala India, working, since 1985 as a non-profit organization, for improvement of houses. It has abled to provide some alternative philosophy and methods for construction of energy-efficient, cost effective houses.

Habitat Technology

Habitat Technology is another similar non-governmental organization, working as nodal agency on the same dimension to carry out green buildings in Kerala.

Major Green Library Initiatives in the world

There are many libraries across the world; those are

working as green libraries. Here some of them are discussed;

Sl. No.	Name of the Library	Initiatives
1.	Fayetteville Public Library, USA	This library was opened to users in the year 2004. It was the first library in Arkansas region that registered for LEED certification and achieved Silver rating. It is believed that the library has become abled to reduce its temperature by 20 degree Celsius with its green roofing system. It is estimated that nearly 25 % energy cost has come down and overall library's energy consume reduced by 30%. Reading spaces and circulation desks were lighted by sunlight during day time.
2.	Blair Library, USA	This library is one of those who registered for U.S. Green Building Council LEED certificate in USA. It came into function in 2006. It is exercising rain water harvesting with its 88,000 sq. ft. roof, low VOC finishes and fabrics. LEED Silver certificate is awarded to it.
3.	The National Library, Singapore	The National library Singapore is considered as the greenest library in this world. The library was designed by Ken Yeang and functioning since 2005. The libraey uses light shelves. It is also the first green library for kids.
4.	Anythink Brighton, Brighton, USA	Anythink Brighton Library is considered as the first carbon negative library in USA. It is believed that annually it saves nearly 30,000 pounds. Library is using geothermal energy for heating and cooling. The library is the recipient of LEED Gold certificate from United Stated Green

		Building Council.
5.	Spanish Peaks Library, Walsenburg, UK	It has adopted geothermal energy for heating and cooling of library. The Library floor has been made of recycled rubber. It received Stephen H Richard award in the year 2010.
6.	Seattle Central Library, USA	Seattle Central Library is the ideal library in terms of site selection. It is said that the library has reduced the transportation cost due to its careful site selection. The library is situated in densely populated area and is harvesting approximate 40,000 gallon water for land irrigation.
7.	University of California, USA	It is reported that due to its green library initiatives, it saves 42% water and 50% energy.
8.	Kanazawa Library, Japan	This library is very special in its own. It has 6000 small circular windows for lighting the library by natural sunlight.
9.	Anna-Centenary Library, India	Thermal insulation glass controlled by solar, library block receives maximus daylight due to certain angle of the library building. It also has green roofing system and use rain water for horticulture to keep the environment green and calm.
10.	IIAS Shimla, India	The library is designed with wood to fix the temperature. It also conserving rain water for greenery purpose.

Advantages of G4G with SDGs

Green library is a kind of special planning of library building which is designed to reduce the harmful effect on the natural environment and increase the quality of inner environment through various ways, for example; logical site selection, use of biodegradable products, use of renewable energy, implementing recycling exercise, adopting conservation water, energy and paper etc. "Green

Library Buildings are not only valuable; it can also serve as excellent vehicles for launching a broader community conservation about environmental issues" (Vijayalakshmi, 2014, 144). We need to understand that building industry (industry which are directly or indirectly associated with the construction of building) is a prominent factor to environmental degradation. Because, these industries produce heat, ash particles, greenhouse gases, destroy natural resources etc. For understanding, "in Canada, buildings consume one third of total energy production, without accounting for the energy used to manufacture and transport building materials. In addition, the building industry in Canada consumes 50% of extracted natural resources, produces 25% of landfill waste, 10% of airborne particulates and 35% of greenhouse gases" (Lackman & Bourdeau, 2008). So, if libraries apply sustainable development goals and implement for themselves, then not only it reduces the negative impact on natural environment but it will be able to show path to others in this regard.The United Nations Environmental Programme (UNEP) points out that the building industry "literally builds the foundations for sustainable development, including housing, workplace, public buildings and services, communications, energy, water and sanitary infrastructures, and provides the context for social interactions as well as economic development at the micro-level"(Lackman&Bourdeau, 2008). As the Green Libraries are environment friendly, hence it will be pleasant and will attract the readers as well. Library will disseminate information to the users and at the same time it will help to keep the mother earth beautiful and pleasant place for the future generations.

CONCLUSION

Day by day our planet is becoming poisonous and unsuitable for living due to several anthropogenic activities. Rapidly increasing greenhouse gases, polluted small particles causes different kinds of diseases to human beings, plants and animals as well. In this juncture, to reduce the dangerous effect, United Nations has taken some initiatives under the Sustainable Development Goals. These goals will help us to make our planet beautiful for us as well as for our future generation. Therefore, to fulfill the objectives of United Nations, IFLA as a pioneer organization of libraries all over the world, advocating the libraries to focus on SDGs. If the libraries follow these goals with responsibility, no doubt we will be able to make awareness which will help to control the harmful effects on environment. Libraries can inspire people to take part at individual and social level to save life, and save earth. Though, green library initiative to achieve SDGs of United Nations is its initial stage. Libraries need to carry out this initiative into mass and wide level; from village to international irrespective of developed, developing and under-developed regions.

REFERENCES

Antonelli, M. (2008).The Green Library Movement: An Overview and Beyond.*UCLA Electronic Green Journal,* 1(27) 12.

Aulisio, G. J. (2013). Green Libraries Are More Than Just Buildings. *Electronic Green Journal, 1*(35). Retrieved from https://escholarship.org/uc/item/3x11862z

Brodie, M. (2012).Building the Sustainable Library at Macquarie University.*Australian Academic & Research Libraries, 43*(1), 4–16. https://doi.org/10.1080/00048623.2012.10722250

Connell, V. (2010). Greening the Library: Collection Development Decisions. *The Journal of the New Members Round Table, 1*(1), 1–15.

Green Building Basics.(n.d.). Retrieved November 23, 2019, from https://www.calrecycle.ca.gov/greenbuilding/basics

Home—2019—United Nations Sustainable Development.(n.d.). Retrieved November 22, 2019, from https://www.un.org/sustainabledevelopment/

Igbinovia, M. (2016). Libraries as Vehicle to Sustainable Developmental Goals (SDGs): Nigerian's current status and outlook. *Library Hi Tech News, 33*(5), 16–17. https://doi.org/10.1108/LHTN-03-2016-0010

Jankowska, M. A., & Marcum, J. W. (2010). Sustainability Challenge for Academic Libraries: Planning for the Future. *College & Research Libraries, 71*(2), 160–170. https://doi.org/10.5860/0710160

Kurbanoðlu, S., &Boustany, J. (2014).From Green Libraries to Green Information Literacy. In S. Kurbanoðlu, S. Špiranec, E. Grassian, D. Mizrachi, & R. Catts (Eds.), *Information Literacy. Lifelong Learning and Digital Citizenship in the 21st Century* (Vol. 492, pp. 47–58). https://doi.org/10.1007/978-3-319-14136-7_6

Lackman, F.-T., &Bourdeau, M. (2008).The advantages of building green | Lexology. Retrieved December 29, 2019, from https://www.lexology.com/library/detail.aspx?g=524e5a22-c059-4e31-a12f-d4f4f8034ead

Malode, M. A. V. (2014). Green Library: An overview. *Research Journey1*(4), 5.

Thomas, R. (2017). Green Libraries: India vs International Scenario.*Scholarly Research Journal for Interdisciplinary Studies, 4*(37). https://doi.org/10.21922/srjis.v4i37.10786

Vijayalakshmi, B. (2014). *Green Library – An Overview.*Presented at International Conference on Library Space and Content Management for Networked Society (IC.LISCOM-2014), Bangalore5.

Woodland, J. (2010). 'Greening' Up the Library.*Community & Junior College Libraries, 16*(4), 241–246. https://doi.org/10.1080/02763915.2010.523325

7

Library in the Horizon of Knowledge Management and Knowledge Harvesting

INTRODUCTION

As we entered into the second decade of 21st century and current period is widely accepted as 'Knowledge Society'. At the same time, there is another terminology which is also very popular namely 'Knowledge as Economy' as a part of knowledge society. These clearly express that knowledge is the most prominent determinant of global economy. The county which has more treasure of knowledge is considered as more influential or vice-versa. So, there is a global race of knowledge either at national, individual or organizational level. As far as organizations and institutions are concerned, knowledge is an inseparable part, knowledge is created and shared to others. In any nation, institution or in an organization, the most precious asset is human resource itselfthat makes all other things/resources work. Nevertheless, organizational learning and management of human resources are not new things to us at all. Subsequently, knowledge of human resource comes out from one's mind.

All the activities, which are taking place at different organizations, institutions or at individual level, are based on the prior data, information and knowledge.

For example, in an organization what are the products, services and resources are developed and manufactured by the human resources based on their prior knowledge that they hold. Therefore, performance of an organization depends on how its human resources can effectively produce knowledge, disseminate this new knowledge and utilize it (Brún, 2005). In simple way it can be said that if the knowledge in any form does not exist within the human minds of organization, then the organization would not be functioning anymore. That is why the concept of knowledge management came into organizational learning domain. Initially, it introduced in business sectors but later it seepages in other domains, for instance library and information science (Agarwal & Islam, 2014). Since the introduction of 'Organization Learning' and 'Knowledge Management', many studies have been done in the last two decades which changed the dimension of these terms and verily the many more development will take place in these domains in coming decades through researches (Easterby-Smith & Lyles, 2011).

According (Brún, 2005)

> (...) knowledge management is surrounded by a great deal of hype. But if you can put the hype to one side, you will find that many of the tools, techniques and processes of knowledge management actually make a great deal of common sense, are already part of what you do, and can greatly help you in your job. (p. 1)

WHAT IS DATA, INFORMATION AND KNOWLEDGE

Before start talking about knowledge management, one should be very clear about the meaning and concept of data, information and knowledge. What kinds of relationship are among them, because, to mean the almost same thing, sometimes we use the term data, sometimes information or knowledge even some cases we use wisdom.

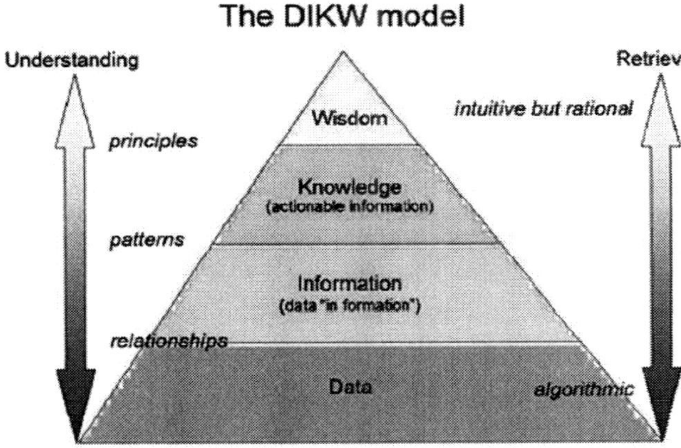

Adopted from (Bird, 2008)

Data : It is any facts, numbers, figures, signs, symbols or anything which is in raw, unorganized and unprocessed and in the first stage to become information. Since, it is raw in nature, unable to express complete meaning. For example, 'black' is a colour, but when we say this word without adding any words with it, then it is meaningless. We cannot have a clear understanding of it whether it is talking about a black umbrella, a black bag or something else. Similarly, if we consider a digit 'two' then it is unable to covey any proper meaning. It may be two men, two cars, two pens or something else. Therefore, the raw and un-organized things are called data. In other way, we may say that data is the first step in the stair of information, where, wisdom is the top step in it.

(Thierauf, 1999) defined data as; "unstructured facts and figures that have the least impact on the typical manager".

Information : Information is the next stage of data, where data become structured, contextualized, classified, organized and able to convey some kinds of meaning. One can say it is categorical or processed data with context and meaning. For example, 'this pen is black' it means a pen is there which is black in colour. It conveys a complete and proper meaning. Normally, we get information in the answers of those question which starts with what, who, when and where (Ackoff, 1999).

Knowledge : It is deep in meaning and vast in area. It is something continuous interpretation, understanding, experience and calculation of past information. In easy way it may be said that knowledge is the answers to the questions which start with how and why. In the stair of information, knowledge is third step next to the information and below to wisdom. For example, if it is said that 'it is raining'. Though the sentence was kind of information but based on past experience, one's knowledge can be able to say, since, it is raining means we need an umbrella if we go outside now otherwise we will get wet.

As Dixon (2000) defined "Knowledge is the meaningful links people make in their minds between information and its application in action in a specific setting".

Wisdom : It is the top most steps in the stair of information. Wisdom is the blending of long experience of knowledge and sharp farsightedness.

TYPES OF KNOWLEDGE

As far as knowledge management is concerned, understanding different kinds of knowledge that exist in and able to identify and differentiate among these types of knowledge is very important. Because, knowledge which is available in a piece of paper has to be managed in a different way from that which knowledge is residing in someone's mind since years. It is found that over the centuries after century philosophers were trying to categorize knowledge and as a result, many distinctions and classification are available based in religion and philosophy (Hajric, 2018).

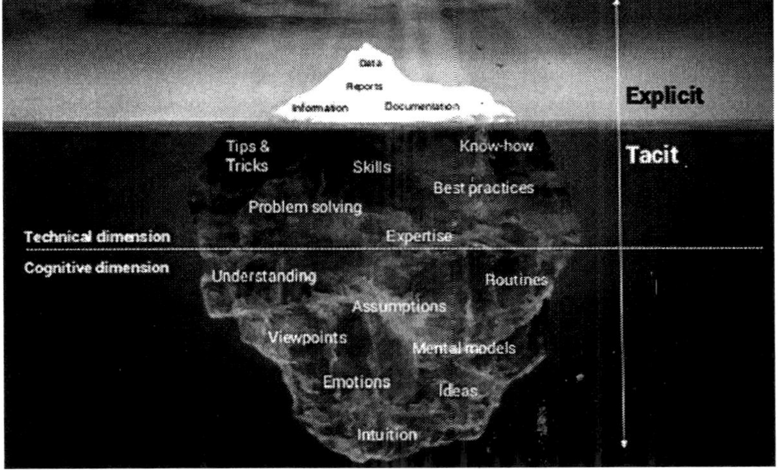

However, in a broad sense and widely accepted way, knowledge has been categorized into two categories ; explicit knowledge and tacit knowledge.

Explicit knowledge : It means articulated knowledge, codified knowledge which is found in different forms of documents, records. One can easily identify, codify, store, documented and retrieve explicit knowledge as well (Wellman, 2009). Usually, this kind of knowledge are the answer of the question 'know-what' and 'know-why'. For example, what is cloud? And why cloud turns into rain? It is easy to answer for a knowledgeable person and also easy to write down and it.

Tacit Knowledge : Tacit knowledge was defined by Polanyi in 1966 for the first time (Hajric, 2018). In contrary to the explicit knowledge, tacit knowledge is difficult to codify and documented. It is residing in mind and gained through experience. This type of knowledge is the answer of the question 'know-how'. For example, how to drive a motor-bike or car?

There is another type of knowledge, available in the

knowledge domain, namely 'implicit knowledge'. This kind of knowledge is considered as the subset of tacit knowledge. There is a very minor and vague difference between tacit and implicit knowledge. As Hanson & Kararach (2011) pointed that implicit knowledge can easily be codified, turned into explicit knowledge.

WHAT IS KNOWLEDGE MANAGEMENT (KM)

Knowledge management is a thriving dimension and method of strategic information management aimed at tackling present challenge in business and organizational sector to develop efficiency and efficacy in already existing strategies, process and knowledge (Agarwal & Islam, 2014). The phase 'knowledge management' itself indicates it has a nexus between knowledge and management. Here it is pertinent to mention that knowledge is the next layer/ stage of information in the data-information and knowledge pyramid. In general, it may be said that knowledge is the meaningful explanation, interpretation of 'know what', 'know why' and 'know how'. On the other side, management is capturing, reorganizing and dissemination for future use. Many of us might be thinking it as a very complex concept although knowingly or unknowingly we all are doing knowledge management in some way or the other. KM is not all about capturing all the available knowledge but storing, articulating and application of important knowledge for an individual or an organization in order to achieve a specific goal (Brún, 2005). It may be at own individual level, institutional level or large level. Knowledge management does not necessarily mean always capturing already existing knowledge and sharing it , but rather it may also include creation of new knowledge and refinement of prior knowledge (Hajric, 2018). Knowledge management system is a set of strategies about how to put knowledge into use as a most important factor in order to add and create value (Alavi & Leidner, 2001; Chua & Banerjee, 2013;

Soto-Acosta & Cegarra-Navarro, 2016). In addition to it, as continuous research and works have been coming out in the field since years which led to bring some modification, addition, conflict and overlapping among the researchers, professionals and practitioners on the concept of knowledge management, but the core idea remain unchanged and still same and equivalent i.e., "managing the knowledge" and stimulate people and organization to disseminate it in order to add value to the services and products (Anand & Singh, 2011). It is worth mentioning here that knowledge management does not mean all about managing knowledge for "*knowledge's sake*". The sole focus is to "*create value and leverage refine the firm's knowledge assets to meet organizational goals*" (Hajric, 2018, 1).

In a precise and simple terms, knowledge management is putting right knowledge at right time in right direction by understanding way of where does knowledge exist, in what form it exist, how it may be useful in future and how to capture and store it.

DEFINITIONS OF KNOWLEDGE MANAGEMENT

There are ample definitions available in different studies and articles about what knowledge management is; here not all but some of those definitions are given below;

"*Knowledge is power, which is why people who had it in the past often tried to make a secret of it. In post-capitalism, power comes from transmitting information to make it productive, not from hiding it!*" -_ (Drucker, 1997)

"*The capability of an organization to create new knowledge, disseminate it throughout the organization and embody it in products, services and systems*"(Nonaka & Takeuchi, 1995)

Skyrme (1997) defines it as:

Knowledge management is the explicit and

systematic management of vital knowledge and its associated processes of creating, gathering, organizing, diffusion, use and exploitation. It requires turning personal knowledge into corporate knowledge that can be widely shared throughout an organization and appropriately applied.

*"Knowledge management is a process that emphasises generating, capturing and sharing information know how and integrating these into business practices and decision making for greater organisational benefit"*_ Maggie Haines, NHS Acting Director of KM

*"The capabilities by which communities within an organisation capture the knowledge that is critical to them, constantly improve it, and make it available in the most effective manner to those people who need it, so that they can exploit it creatively to add value as a normal part of their work"*_ BSI's A Guide to Good Practice in KM

BRIEF HISTORY OF KNOWLEDGE MANAGEMENT

It is found, the connotation KM as a conscious area of study, to be appeared somewhere in 1990s (Brún, 2005) but its actual root is much more deeper and it is believed that from the idea of different academicians, practitioners such as, Management Guru, Peter Drucker it evolved in 1970s (Brún, 2005). Successively, Karl-Erik Sveiby, 1980s, Nonanka and Takeuchi in the 1990s appeared (Brún, 2005). During 1990s, a shift was noticed in the working, social and economic behaviour among the companies from what they used to. Another important thing at that period was that globalization entered into arena which opened new horizon of opportunities but on the other hand it is fact that it brought wide race in the national and international level (Brún, 2005).

In fact, in 1990s large chunk of academicians, professionals, practitioners, consultants and managers started talking emphatically about this new strategy of management (knowledge management). Eventually, number of research papers, works begin to come up in journals and conferences around the world. Therefore, in mid 1990s it became widely accepted technique of managing knowledge in the business and organizational domain and abled to take a significant position in business atmosphere, till today it is not only intact but rather increasing and spreading to other domains as well (Brún, 2005). Here, we categorized the journey (since 1990 to till date) of knowledge management into four generation with some modification to the approaches of Anand & Singh (2011), who categorized it into three sections.

First Generation (1990-1995) : the beginning phase includes introducing the definitions of Knowledge Management, impacts of KM on business, proposed various projects of knowledge management and some of the studies are (Harris, 1990; Nonaka et al., 1996; Quinn, 1992; Wiig, 1993).

Second Generation (1996-2000) : in this stage different application of KM onto business, role of KM in business and organizational development, introducing of KM frameworks, executions process of KM and some of the studies are (Alavi & Leidner, 2001; Grant, 1997; Holsapple & Joshi, 2002 and Rajan, Lank & Chapple, 1999).

Third Generation (2001 - 2010) : though Anand & Singh (2011) placed technical advancement in the second generation of KM but here we felt better to place as the beginning of third generation instead of. Further, they included artificial intelligence in the first generation but here again unlike them placing the introduction of artificial intelligence in KM in the third generation. No doubt in it that some ideas were there about artificial intelligence in 1990s but not up to satisfied level. Besides those, converting knowing into action is also in third generation as suggested by (Anand & Singh, 2011). Some of the studies related to this category are (Carneiro, 2001; Liao, 2003; Paraponaris, 2003).

Fourth Generation (2011-2019) : As we mentioned earlier that, although, the concept of knowledge management was introduced in the business domain, but with time it is now no more limited within the boundary of business and industry rather it is spreading into different non-profit organizations like libraries. Hence, in the fourth generation we are applying KM dimensions in to others fields and latest technological development for example application of artificial intelligence, application Internet of Things (IoT), and use of social media in KM etc. The examples of few studies which have taken place in this stage are (Husain & Nazim, 2015; Imran et al., 2019; Kumar & Islam, 2014; Obeidat et al., 2016; Soto-Acosta & Cegarra-Navarro, 2016; Wai Tat & Hase, 2007).

The categorization of knowledge management was shown in a table with generations and periodic studies;

Sl. No	*Research Areas of KM*	*Generations*	*Authors of Studies*
1.	Basics/ fundamentals of KM	1st Gen	Liebowitz & Beckman, 1998; Wiig, 1993)
2.	Knowledge creation and process	1st Gen	(Nonaka et al., 1996; Nonaka et al., 1996)
3.	Arts of KM, developments of KM	1st Gen	(Quinn, 1992; Senge, 2006)
4.	KM in Business Development	2nd Gen	(Grant, 1997; Thierauf, 1999)
5.	Framework and Execution of KM	2nd Gen	(Alavi &Leidner, 2001; Rajan, Lank, & Chapple, 1999)
6.	Impact of KM	2nd Gen	(Rowley, 1999)
7.	Artificial intelligence and KM	3rd Gen	(Fowler, 2000; Grundspenkis & Kirikova, 2005 and Liebowitz (2001)
8.	KM and decision making; issues of KM	3rd Gen	(Bolloju et al., 2002; Courtney, 2001 and King, 2009)

9.	KM and technology (initial stage)	3rd Gen	(Mc Adam and Reid, 2001; Tyndale, 2002; and Wong & Aspinwall, 2004)
10.	ICT and KM	4th Gen	(Archer-Brown & Kietzmann, 2018; Imran et al., 2019; Panahi et al., n.d., 2013; Soto-Acosta & Cegarra-Navarro, 2016)
11.	KM in Library	4th Gen	(Husain & Nazim, 2015; Kumar Agarwal & Anwarul Islam, 2014; Roknuzzaman & Umemoto, 2013; Sarrafzadeh et al., 2010)
12.	KM in Aerospace and other fields	4th Gen	(Inkinen, 2016; Obeidat et al., 2016; Wai Tat & Hase, 2007)

NEED KNOWLEDGE MANAGEMENT

As we mentioned that knowledge is the most vital resource in any organization which resides in human brain. Therefore, first priority is human intellect followed by the people of organization.It also said that knowledge management is not a new concept at all rather it is a changing pattern of human resources. Earlier, focus was laid upon *"human power"* but now the focal point is knowledge of human. In knowledge society, it is verily clear that knowledge is involved in every activity from bottom to top. That is why; there is a need of management of knowledge.

Here, we tried to explain the necessity of knowledge management with some examples; in the perspective of library, the relationship between librarians and users are not as it was in old days, the demand of the users arealso changing and eventually it varies from user to user.On the other side, constantly new developments are taking place in science and technology. Therefore, as a librarian when he or she will be trying to be abreast with new developments in the science and technology, when he/

she will be discussing the various problems of users and their different types demands, when that librarian will be approaching to provide enhanced services to the users, that librarian must have acquired some new knew knowledge during these learning process which will make him/her expert on that particular area. Now, imagine, if that librarian get retired, it does not mean that librarian only get retired himself. In practical sense, all knowledge went missing with that librarian. And who will be his/her successor will have to follow the same practice for that same kind of knowledge and it will go on. Therefore, knowledge management is essential so that with the retirement of one's knowledge does not go away and same activities need no to repeatedly doing. So that organization can resume that service from where the earlier one has finished and not to start from the beginning. Similarly, in medical context, the already existing knowledge of a doctor is not enough forever because, different new diseases are coming out, new researches are taking place, situation is changing, and behaviour (life-style) is changing. Therefore, doctors have to be well versed with the new knowledge as well as with new technology for diagnosing patients accordingly. And when doctor will do these jobs he or she will be gaining new knowledge. And for the same reason, it should be managed to save time, to give the organization a dynamic momentum (Brún, 2005).

Here, one more interesting thing to be noticed that many times, we either in our offices or homes or at any workplace, do some recording/documentation or note down our important things but later when it is again needed, we do not find or it takes too much time to get that information out. In this regard, it is pertinent to uncover what according to (Brún, 2005) working professionals spend ten percent of their time in finding information which already they noticed, recorded or kept somewhere. Let's say, we noticed a piece of information to a particular person few days back and now we are in need of that specific information. What will happen if that person is not available at the same place where we saw him/her last time,because neither human beings are always available around us nor they can be fixed/posted at one place for all time. So, if we do not do the articulation of knowledge, storing of knowledge, management of knowledge at right time, then it will be very difficult to do that later or when it will be needed. In the study by Alavi & Leidner (2001) showed that in most of the cases, needed knowledge is existed in the organization itself but the problem is to identifying, locating and leveraging, maintaining them, which shows the necessity of a systematic knowledge management. According to Davenport &Prusak (1998) and Hajric(2018) in any organization, knowledge management initiative must have at least one of these few objectives:

1. Knowledge, wherever it is existing (may be in some particular department, in one expert's mind, with a team or in an old document) in the organization, has to be made visible to all and highlighting the significance of knowledge in the organization through different techniques and tools.
2. Identify the form of knowledge means in what form it is, whether it is in the mind of people or in a piece of paper or in some other forms.
3. There has to build a 'knowledge-intensive culture' among the organization either by motivating, encouraging the people or making them proactive to share, to offer and to seek knowledge.
4. A knowledge-infrastructure must be developed there with the application of all kinds of technologies to create efficiency and efficacy among the people who are engaged with.
5. Methodically, need to evaluate the organizational existing knowledge vs organization's need and do act accordingly for example, "by hiring or firing" or

"promoting specific in-house knowledge creation".

Therefore, in a very concise way, we may say that knowledge management is needed either at individual level or organizational level to keep right knowledge at right place and provide right knowledge to the right person to the right direction at right time.

PRINCIPLES AND MODELS OF KM

Knowledge management is the strategic mechanism to manage knowledge. When we say knowledge management, there are some principles and strategies which describe how to manage and way to manage knowledge in an organization. In this context, it is found that most of the scholars believed that strategy of knowledge management is a dichotomy in nature i.e. codification vs personalization (Buenechea-Elberdin et al., 2018; López-Nicolás & Meroño-Cerdán, 2011).

Codification : in other way we may term it as explicit strategy. Codification strategy is written down or capturing the explicit knowledge (easily expressible) in documents or databases and it is easy to access and communicate among others in the company or firms. It can be documented or shared in spreadsheets, numbers, formulae, words etc. The codification strategy or explicit knowledge can furthered be categorized as structured and un-structured. When explicit knowledge is codified in databases, spreadsheet or documents is termed as structured codification, while on the other side, if it is codified in the form of image, email, training course etc. is considered as un-structured codification.

Personalisation : similarly, it is also known as tacit strategy. This strategy is applicable for tacit knowledge which is not easy to share or recorded because, this type of knowledge is "less concrete" and somewhat "unspoken understanding". People use to carry it for a long time. It includes "subjective insights, intuitions, and hunches" "not easily visible and expressible" and "highly personal and hard to formalize" as well. Thus, the strategy, which is used to manage this type of knowledge, is person-to-person, conversation amongst the people, discussion in workshop, meeting or in an informal talk.

Knowing what you know : it is a kind of strategy related to the already existed knowledge in the institution. The old knowledge or knowing what you know means finding out the knowledge which they know and then articulate that knowledge to circulate or communicate amongst all the people of the company. It is the first step in regard of knowledge management. Many experts believe, if we can manage what we know effectively and efficiently, then most of the problem of a company will be solved. Thus, mapping of knowledge flows of organizational knowledge and conduction of audit might be the useful approach in order to manage old knowledge.

Creating new knowledge : in converse to knowing what you know, it is somehow related to the tacit knowledge of personal strategy. It is the next level of strategy to manage knowledge in the firm. Once the already existed knowledge gets managed, then there is a need of creating new knowledge. Creating new knowledge is not always necessarily R&D activities, but rather hiring experts, organizing inter organization discussion forums, seminars, workshops where experts from different institutions will share their knowledge, discuss together which leads to creation of new knowledge (Brún, 2005).

MODELS

For almost each strategy there are some models and frameworks because, a model can show the different relationship and significance among various elements. Similarly, knowledge management has also number of models and frameworks given by different scholars at different time and perspective. As knowledge management is an interdisciplinary as well as multidisciplinary aspect (Husain & Nazim, 2015), so the models and frameworks also vary from one to another. Apart from this, problem of knowledge management is not same everywhere and every organization, it is differs from organization to organization. Further, the need of knowledge management also depends company to company. That is why all the models neither same in meaningfully nor purposefully but, all the models are some way or the other dependent and affected by multiple factors. Thus, the models are bit difficult. Here are discussing about some of the models of knowledge management.

SECI MODEL BY (NONAKA & TAKEUCHI, 1996)

This model came out in the research of (Nonaka & Takeuchi, 1996). It is not only related to knowledge management but it also relates with organizational learning, information management and business administration. It is one of the most widely accepted and cited model in the domain of knowledge management which explains creation of knowledge, transformation tacit knowledge to explicit and vice-versa in a firm. It has for dimensions; socialization (tacit to tacit), externalization (tacit to explicit), combination (explicit to explicit) and internalization (explicit to tacit).

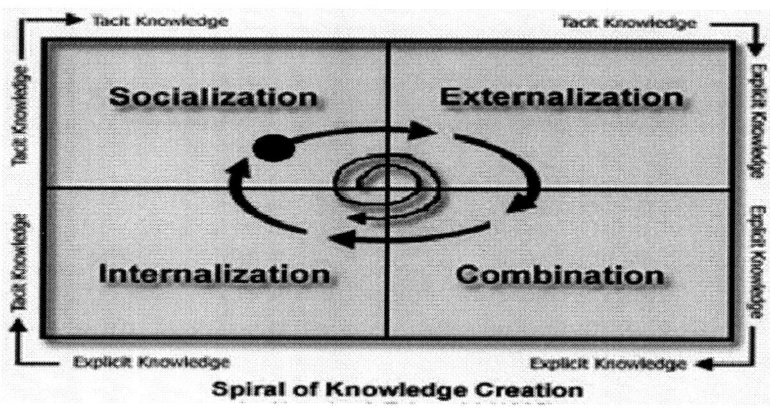

SECI Model (Nonaka et al., 1996)

Socialization : this dimension includes tacit to tacit

knowledge that describes the social interaction happens with the process of tacit to tacit knowledge communication. Since, tacit knowledge is difficult to codify and documented hence, tacit knowledge can be shared person to person or face to face through discussion, spending time together or brain storming. Socialization for example hands-on training and experience can help in transferring tacit knowledge.

Externalization : in this dimension formalizing, articulating, publishing of tacit knowledge takes place and turned into explicit knowledge. When through discussion, creating concept map, and sharing experience are codified in a document then tacit knowledge gets crystalized, thus it leads to creates new knowledge.

Combination : combination refers to the accumulation of different explicit knowledge either from inside organization or outside organizations and reorganized, processed to create a new knowledge.

Internalization : here a person in an organization receives explicit knowledge and applies that in his/her job and learns new knowledge. In other way, based on documented knowledge he/she will develop a new type of expertise. Thus, new expertise is tacit knowledge for an organization.

It is a circular model which will continuously has to be happened in any company to manage knowledge (to manage old knowledge as well as to manage new knowledge).

KNOWLEDGE MANAGEMENT MATRIX BY (GAMBLE & BLACKWELL, 2001)

This is a general as well as theoretical model but it gives specific guidelines to implement KM project in any organization. The model is having four levels; sense (locate/find out) is the first stage where knowledge has to be identified and located. The identified and stored knowledge has to be gone through different assessment, evaluation and organization process in order to codified and documented, which is considered as the second level. Socialize is the third stage that includes several techniques to add a value in it to make it useful to others in the organization and followed by internalize process where knowledge gets internalized through its use and application.

Type / Approach	Embodied	Represented	Embedded
Sense	Observe	Gather	Hypothesize
Organize	Contextualize	Categorize	Map
Socialize	Share	Disseminate	Simulate
Internalize	Apply, Decide, Act		

KM Matrix by (Gamble & Blackwell, 2001)

THE KNOWLEDGE MANAGEMENT PROCESS MODEL BY BOTHA ET AL (2008)

This model is believed as a realist model of knowledge management where, three broad categories exist and they are interacting with each other but in technical sense, these three categories are the intermingling of four stages which were shown in previous model. The model focuses on strategic knowledge so "know why" and "know how" as opposed to "know what is omitted. The important thing to be noticed in this model is that both the dichotomy (codification vs personalisation and knowing what they know vs creating new knowledge) have been take care into this model.

It also shows that KM is more and more people oriented and technology focused. Although focusing on technology is a debatable issue but of course, technology has a significant role in KM initiative.

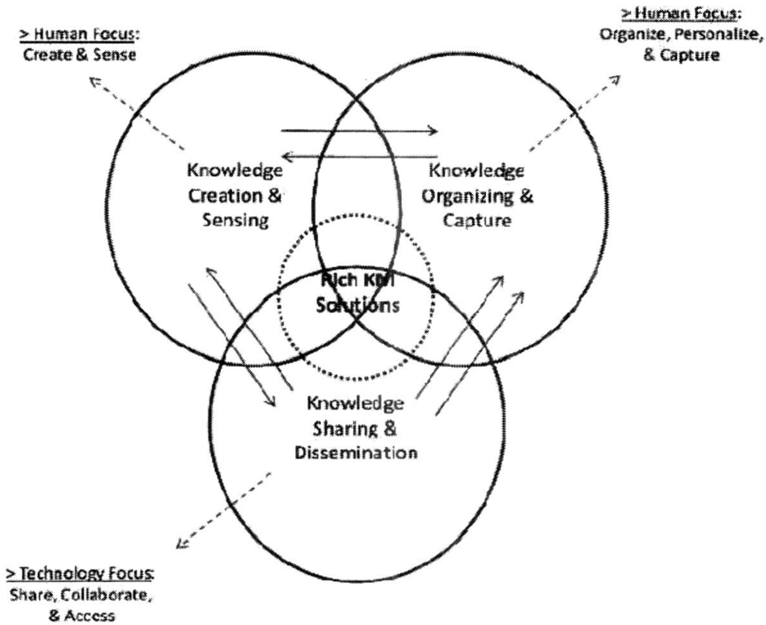

KM Model by Botha et al (2008)

KM CYCLE

Knowledge management in library means it will manage the knowledge exist around the library itself as well as knowledge of entire institution. From the discussion of various scholars such as (Agarwal & Islam, 2011; Dalkir, 2011 and Townley, 2001). Knowledge management is a circular strategy which constitutes number of phases for example, identification, codification, capture, creation, sharing and application of knowledge by the needy. As (Agarwal & Islam, 2014)perpetuated eight phases that encompasses a good knowledge management strategy;

1. Knowledge creation.
2. Knowledge acquisition or sourcing.
3. Knowledge compilation or capture.
4. Knowledge organization, refinement, transformation and storage.
5. Knowledge dissemination, transfer and access.
6. Knowledge learning and application.
7. Knowledge evaluation and value realization.
8. Knowledge reuse or divesting.

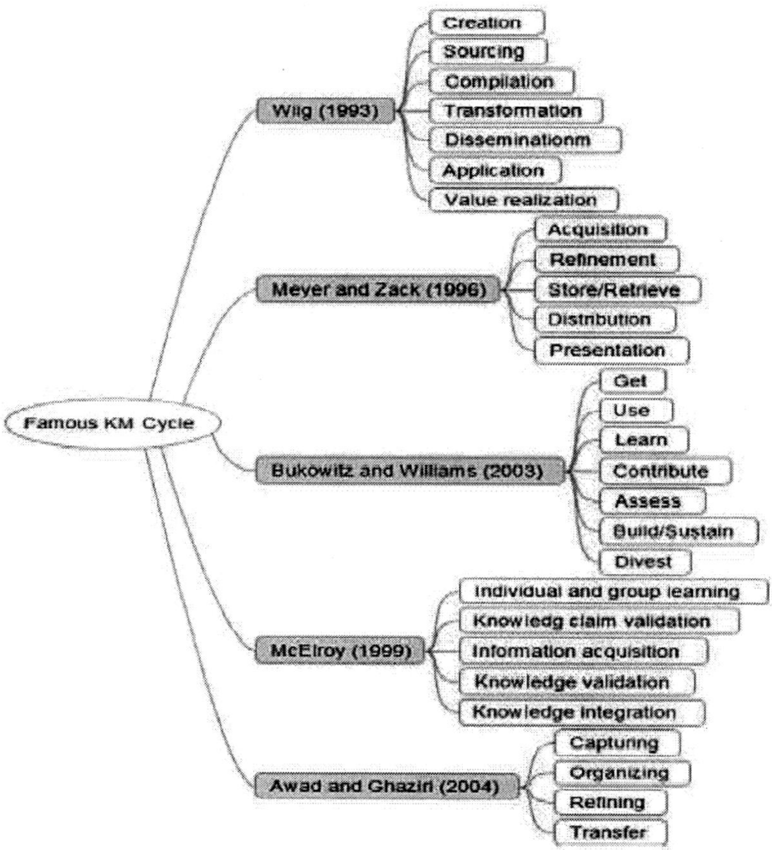

Adopted from (Agarwal & Islam, 2014)

DEVELOPING KM ENVIRONMENT

In general, the environment of knowledge management is based on three aspects; people (human resource), process and technology. In order to develop Km environment, organization has to identify if there is any hurdle and possibility. Further, it should remove the obstacle and try to give a shape to that possibility on ground. These three should work together in a same direction to make knowledge management environment a useful and effective.

People : in any firm irrespective of type, purpose and location, universally, the most important element out of these three is people because, it is the people who create knowledge, share knowledge and make use of knowledge too. All the things in an organization are getting done around us is directly or indirectly by people. Process and technology are only assisting elements to make the job happen in a better way and least time. But at the end of the day, all the works depend on knowledge of people either will do it or not. Many companies did not believe it even still many of them do not. Contrary to it, many companies started to realise, after heavy investing on latest and trendy process and technology which became futile, that it is human resource may "make or break" KM environment or initiatives.

First of all, in an institution for developing knowledge management environment, behaviour of human (top to bottom level), should be knowledge sharing rather only becoming knowledgeable person. It has found that people have some misbelieves, due to that attitude there exist anti-knowledge sharing, which needs to be changed. Few examples of old and misbelieves are "person who poses more knowledge is more powerful, I do not have enough time to share, that is not my job, what is in it for me, "I would like to assist you, but my boss do not want I invest my time for another team where I do not belong to", " we are not allowed to make mistakes, let alone admit to them, share them or learn from them", don not irritate others by asking them for assistance, and "work it out for yourself" etc.

Organizational culture and Individual behaviour : Knowledge sharing is in fact very common phenomenon which we see around us such as on phone, at public discussion, by email we get people to share their knowledge to others but this not the normal phenomenon as far as office, organization and firms are concerned. There may be two prominent factors which are responsible for the abnormal occurrence; organizational culture and individual behaviour.

Organizational culture : in our society, from the school age, sharing of knowledge, use of someone else' knowledge is treated as cheating and this way we are habituated to thinking of it. In company, individual efforts are given much more importance over the team work and thus, a tendency of individual competition exists in the firms. Organizational culture means "the way we do things around here". Companies recognize individual achievements even people are rewarded for their individual knowledge but unfortunately there are no incentives for the sharing of knowledge, team achievements and team efforts. This kind of organizational culture conceived as barriers of KM environment. Therefore, the things we need focus on to remove this conception are;

- creation, sharing and use of knowledge are integral part of institution's culture,
- teams within company should co-operate each other rather than competing each other,
- Knowledge should be made open for all; anyone can use it, contribute to it or share it to others,
- Administration of the institution should emphasize on knowledge rather than individual, and
- rewards, incentives and appraisals should be given for knowledge sharing and using of knowledge as well.

Individual behaviour : when institutional culture will be turned into pro-knowledge sharing rather than knowledge gaining, then the individual behaviour of the staff will become a significant factor. Whether people are sharing their knowledge, co-operating as team-work, better performance being a team, learning from others' experience and knowledge, approaching to the experts among the institution or not. Are all the staff participating collectively in organizational achievement, developing new heights? Like organizational culture, here also some measures need to be taken care of in order to change individual behaviour;

- Institution should introduce its policies, decisions and objectives among the staff
- Encouraging the people for collaborative work
- Organization should make its human resources understood about its culture
- Institution should listen to all (staff) irrespective of their position
- It should recognize and reward the staff in various ways
- Institution should promote those people who are expert, who share knowledge more than the other, who collaborate more with others, as champions and heroes around the organizations to motivate others.

DEVELOPING KM STRATEGY

"A Knowledge management strategy is simply a plan that describes how an organization will manage its knowledge better for the benefit of that organisations and its stakeholders." A sound strategy should always closely be aligned with the institutional aims and objectives. Thus, to make a strategy good enough, it should keep in mind the three points;

1. Where are we now : it is all about the assessment of on-going situation of the company. How does KM work going on? Whether it is practicing as per the expectation or it is lacking somewhere? Is it able to achieve organizational goal? Do the organizational culture, process, and technology are working "as enabler of, or barriers to" a sound KM initiatives.

2. Where do we want to be : what will be the objectives and goals (short term and long term goals) of the organization? What will be the action plan for different teams and overall all institutions as well.

3. How do we get there : how can we achieve the target? How can we fulfil libraries objectives and mission? How can we build supportive infrastructure? What will be required resources and skills?

SOCIAL MEDIA IN KNOWLEDGE MANAGEMENT

When web 2.0 is installed in an organization, is termed as organization 2.0 and further the use of 2.0 in KM is considered as KM 2.0 (Hajric, 2018). Social media tools are a prototype of technology that is a very significant aspect in the process of knowledge management. Thus, the role of social media comes under use of technology in knowledge management (Forcier et al., 2013). Library can use social media as service tools where users will get the opportunity to exchange knowledge with librarian as well as with other users. For example, Princeton Public Library uses blogs and wikis, where users posted about books reviews and recommendations which are found to be pretty useful for other users (Forcier et al., 2013). Martin Niemi & Greatbanks (2010) discoursed that "blogs have potential to develop communities with all of the attributes necessary to provide environment for tacit-to-tacit as well as individual-to-collective knowledge conversion"(p.21). Hence, social media can play an important role in knowledge management (KM) practices.

Social media supports knowledge management practices : In the epoch of Web 2.0, social media tools are playing a vital role in socialization and it is worth

mentioning that socialization is believed as one of the core task among the employees of a firm or non-profit organizations to eliminate the "bottlenecks of knowledge management". Apart from this, there are few social media tools that are considered as knowledge providers(Imran et al., 2019).Employees make use of social media in order to enhance internal knowledge and exchange among others. Perceived usefulness of SM tools in terms of knowledge codification, articulation and share are highly noticeable.

Social media-a component of ICT not only support in sharing and exchanging knowledge among the organizations but it can create individual as well as organizational knowledge. Social media has also provided the opportunity to collaborate with experts from different places to create and develop new knowledge.

Social media supports the resource knowledge : Social media not only helps in managing various types of knowledge butit contributes in improving overall quality of knowledge as well. It is a major assisting tool to improve the quality of relational, structural and social knowledge. It also assists in making communication process more visible and faster, which in turn contribute the institutions in the mechanism of KM.

Social media helps in overcoming knowledge management barriers : Social media makes the process of KM easier by providing the facility to share information about the experts, affiliation and expertise. Social media helps to provide information from anywhere at any time around the world.As Imran et al. (2019)described that social media has become able to strike down all the barriers in knowledge exchange and become able to provide active vehicle to share and exchange of internal as well as external knowledge. No doubt, to what extent SM tools are useful, to reduce the bottlenecks of KM practice and to foster knowledge sharing, acquiring and exchange of knowledge, is a debatable issue.

KNOWLEDGE HARVESTING

Knowledge harvesting is not a different thing rather it is an inseparable techniques associated with KM strategy (Serrat, 2010). Knowledge harvesting is categorically a similar strategy as water harvesting. The steps of water harvesting are :first water is stored then it is cleansed if it is dirty then it is used for different purposes. Similarly, in terms of knowledge harvesting, first knowledge is articulated and stored, then it is processed and repackaged and finally the knowledge is made accessible for all to make best use of it. Knowledge management is typically the exercise of gathering and packaging of institutional tacit knowledge in order to help others by applying that knowledge in creating of innovating something in future (Pierson, 2013). The purpose of KM harvesting is not to store and capture all the knowledge randomly. Instead, it will capture and repackaged all those knowledge keeping in mind the institutional goal.

Hanson & Kararach (2011) and Serrat (2010) perpetuated seven approaches to knowledge harvesting i.e. 'focus', 'finding critical positions', 'eliciting correct feedbacks', 'organizing the knowledge', 'packaging and dissemination', 'evaluation' and 'adapting the knowledge'.

According to Hanson &Kararach (2011)there are certain points which need to be taken care of as to exercise knowledge harvesting.These are (i) a given KM strategy is understood by all and with management buy-in; (ii) one identifies and taps the knowledge resources available especially–staff know-how, information resources, technology and their links to stakeholders; (iii) there is development of a culture premised on continuous learning, openness, productive co-operation, knowledge sharing and diversity of 'knowers'; and (iv) there are appropriate knowledge capture, conversion and dissemination tools & techniques(p.7).

One should be very clear, before approaching

knowledge harvesting in library or in any organizations, that whether that firm or institution's culture is pro-knowledge sharing or discourages to share knowledge. If the culture says that staff will get more advantages whoever will keep their tacit knowledge to themselves. Because, pro-knowledge sharing culture is pre-requisite for healthy knowledge harvesting as well as knowledge management practice.

BENEFITS OF KNOWLEDGE MANAGEMENT

As the rate of creation, producing and sharing of informationhas tremendously increased but at the same time, the life span of information has significantly reduced. Thus, managing of information and knowledge in organization as well as in library has become undoubtedly essential (see; why KM is needed). When we say KM is an essential strategy, then it must have some advantages and of course disadvantages too. The benefits of knowledge management in a library or an organization are drawn here;

1. Accumulation of KM : as storing is a stage of KM hence, it will gather all types (tacit and explicit) of knowledge that available in that institution which itself is a great achievement.

2. Accessibility of KM : Since all knowledge will be stored and organized and will be made available for all the staff and users as of when they need it.

3. Quick exchange of KM : The prime object of KM initiative is to provide right knowledge at right time to the right person at right direction. It means knowledge will be shared at right time without any delay.

4. Faster decision making : Circulation of right knowledge at right time will surely help to take decision making at right time which is very important.

5. Foster new innovation : If a library or an organization becomes able to hold knowledge of its staff and make it for all users and people then it will be helpful for others to create something new by using available knowledge.

6. Improve service quality : Particularly in terms of library, KM practice will help to add value and quality to the service of library.

CONCLUSION

Due to the immense importance of KM in our organizations, irrespective of profit making or non-profit making, it has gained a shape of full-fledged discipline and many institutional courses are offered at graduated level (Husain & Nazim, 2015). Despite of the great significance of KM, in our LIS education and profession the focus on KM is compromisable. However, a gradual improvement is noticed at different LIS institutions and working professions. But, still LIS education should include KM in its curriculum and should give due importance to it. It should build an interdisciplinary collaboration with other institutional organs for the better improvement on KM.

REFERENCES

Ackoff, R.L. (1989). From data to wisdom.*Journal of Applied Systems Analysis*, 16, 3-9.

Alavi, M., & Leidner, D. E. (2001). Review: Knowledge Management and Knowledge Management Systems: Conceptual Foundations and Research Issues. *MIS Quarterly, 25*(1), 107. https://doi.org/10.2307/3250961

Anand, A., & Singh, M. D. (2011). Understanding Knowledge Management: A literature review. *International Journal of Engineering Science and Technology, 3*(2), 14.

Archer-Brown, C., & Kietzmann, J. (2018). Strategic knowledge management and enterprise social media. *Journal of Knowledge Management, 22*(6), 1288–1309. https://doi.org/10.1108/JKM-08-2017-0359

Bird, C. (2008). Are you searching for ways to find information. *Proceedings of the 22nd British HCI Group Annual Conference on HCI 2008: People and Computers XXII: Culture, Creativity, Interaction, 2.* https://doi.org/10.1145/1531826.1531901

Bolloju, N., Khalifa, M. and Turban, E. (2002). Integrating Knowledge Management into enterprise environments for the next generation decision support. *Decision Support Systems*, 33, 163-76.

Botha, A., Kourie, D., & Snyman, R. (2008). Coping with Continuous Change in the Business Environment: Knowledge Management and Knowledge Management Technology. Oxford, UK: Chandos Publishing

Brún, C. D. (2005). *ABC of Knowledge Management.* NHS National Library for Health: Knowledge Management Specialist Library. http://www.library.nhs.uk/knowledge management/

Buenechea-Elberdin, M., Sáenz, J., & Kianto, A. (2018). Knowledge management strategies, intellectual capital, and innovation performance: A comparison between high- and low-tech firms. *Journal of Knowledge Management, 22*(8), 1757–1781. https://doi.org/10.1108/JKM-04-2017-0150

Carneiro, A. (2001). The role of intelligent resources in Knowledge Management. *Journal of Knowledge Management*, 5(4), 358-67.

Chua, A. Y. K., & Banerjee, S. (2013). Customer knowledge management via social media: The case of Starbucks. *Journal of Knowledge Management, 17*(2), 237–249. https://doi.org/10.1108/13673271311315196

Courtney, J. (2001). Decision making and Knowledge Management in inquiring organizations: toward a new decision-making paradigm for DSS. *Decision Support Systems*, 31(1), 17-38.

Dalkir, K. (2011), *Knowledge Management in Theory and Practice*, 2nd ed., MIT Press, Cambridge, MA.

Davenport, T.H. and Prusak, L. (1998) *Working Knowledge: How Organizations Manage What They Know.* Harvard Business School Press, Boston.

Dixon, N. M. (2000) *Common knowledge: How companies thrive by sharing what they know*, Harvard Business School Press, Boston, Massachusetts.

Drucker, P. F. (1997). *Managing in a time of great change.* Butterworth-Heinemann. http://public.ebookcentral.proquest.com/choice/publicfullrecord.aspx?p=1039317

Easterby-Smith, M., & Lyles, M. A. (Eds.). (2011). *Handbook of organizational learning and knowledge management* (2nd ed). Wiley.

Fowler, A. (2000). The role of AI-based technology in support of the Knowledge Management value activity cycle. *Journal of Strategic Information Systems*, 9, 107-28.

Forcier, E., Rathi, D., & Given, L. M. (2013). Knowledge Management and Social Media: A Case Study of Two Public Libraries in Canada. *Journal of Information & Knowledge Management*, *12*(04), 1350039. https://doi.org/10.1142/S0219649213500391

Gamble, P. R., & Blackwell, J. (2001). *Knowledge management: A state of the art guide/ ; models & tools, strategy, intellectual capital, planning, learning, culture, processes*. Kogan Page.

Grant, R. M. (1997). The knowledge-based view of the firm: Implications for management practice. *Long Range Planning*, *30*(3), 450–454. https://doi.org/10.1016/S0024-6301(97)00025-3

Grundspenkis, J., & Kirikova, M. (2005). Impact of the Intelligent Agent Paradigm on Knowledge Management. In C. T. Leondes (Ed.), *Intelligent Knowledge-Based Systems* (pp. 164–206). Springer US. https://doi.org/10.1007/978-1-4020-7829-3_7

Hajric, E. (2018). Knowledge Management.pdf—Knowledge Management System and Practices A Theoretical and Practical Guide for Knowledge Management in Your Organization. Retrieved January 27, 2020, fromhttps://www.coursehero.com/file/44877187/Knowledge-Managementpdf/

Hanson, K. T., & Kararach, G. (2011). *The challenges of knowledge harvesting and the promotion of sustainable development for the achievement of the MDGS in Africa*. African Capacity Building Foundation.

Harris, S. G. (1990). The fifth discipline: The art and practice of the learning organization, by Peter Senge, New York: Doubleday/Currency, 1990. *Human Resource Management*, *29*(3), 343–348. https://doi.org/10.1002/hrm.3930290308

Husain, S., & Nazim, M. (2015). Exploring the need of knowledge management education within library and information science educational courses: An Indian perspective. *New*

Library World, 116(11/12), 711–727. https://doi.org/10.1108/NLW-07-2015-0051

Holsapple, C., & Joshi, K.D. (2002). Knowledge Management: a threefold framework. *The Information Society,* 18(1), 47–64.

Imran, M. K., Iqbal, S. M. J., Aslam, U., & Fatima, T. (2019). Does social media promote knowledge exchange? A qualitative insight. *Management Decision, 57*(3), 688–702. https://doi.org/10.1108/MD-05-2017-0477

Inkinen, H. (2016). Review of empirical research on knowledge management practices and firm performance. *Journal of Knowledge Management, 20*(2), 230–257. https://doi.org/10.1108/JKM-09-2015-0336

King, W. R. (2009). Knowledge Management and Organizational Learning. In W. R. King (Ed.), *Knowledge Management and Organizational Learning,* 4, 3–13. Springer US. https://doi.org/10.1007/978-1-4419-0011-1_1

Kumar Agarwal, N., & Anwarul Islam, M. (2014). Knowledge management implementation in a library: Mapping tools and technologies to phases of the KM cycle. *VINE, 44*(3), 322–344. https://doi.org/10.1108/VINE-01-2014-0002

Liebowitz, J. (2001).Knowledge Management and its links to artificial intelligence. *Expert Systems with Applications,* 20, 1-6.

Liebowitz. J., & Beckm, T. (1998). Knowledge Organizations: What every manager should know. USA, St. Lucie Press.

López-Nicolás, C., & Meroño-Cerdán, Á. L. (2011). Strategic knowledge management, innovation and performance. *International Journal of Information Management, 31*(6), 502–509. https://doi.org/10.1016/j.ijinfomgt.2011.02.003

Martin Niemi, F., & Greatbanks, R. (2010). The ba of blogs: Enabling conditions for knowledge conversion in blog communities. *VINE,* 40(1), 7–23. https://doi.org/10.1108/03055721011024892

Mary Ellen Pierson, Virginia Tech. (2013). Characteristics of a Knowledge Harvesting and Management System. *TechTrends, 57*(2), 26–32. https://doi.org/10.1007/s11528-013-0642-4

Mc Adam, R., & Reid, R. (2001). SME and large organization perceptions of Knowledge Management: comparisons and contrasts. *Journal of Knowledge Management,* 5 (3), 231-41.

Nonaka. I., & Takeuchi, M. (1995). *The knowledge creating company-how Japanese companies create the dynamics of innovation.* Oxford: The Oxford University press.

Nonaka, lkujiro, Takeuchi, H., & Umemoto, K. (1996). A theory of organizational knowledge creation. *International Journal of Technology Management, 11*(7–8), 833–845.

Nonaka, I., Umemoto, K., & Senoo, D. (1996). From Information Processing to Knowledge Creation:A Paradigm Sm in Business Management. *Technology in Society, 18*(2), 203–218.

Obeidat, B. Y., Al-Suradi, M. M., Masa'deh, R., & Tarhini, A. (2016). The impact of knowledge management on innovation: An empirical study on Jordanian consultancy firms. *Management Research Review, 39*(10), 1214–1238. https://doi.org/10.1108/MRR-09-2015-0214

Panahi, S., Watson, J., & Partridge, H. (n.d.). *Social Media and Tacit Knowledge Sharing: Developing a Conceptual Model.* 9.

Panahi, S., Watson, J., & Partridge, H. (2013). Towards tacit knowledge sharing over social web tools. *Journal of Knowledge Management, 17*(3), 379–397. https://doi.org/10.1108/JKM-11-2012-0364

Quinn, J. B. (1992). The Intelligent Enterprise a New Paradigm. *The Executive, 6*(4), 48–63. JSTOR.

Rajan, A., Lank, E., & Chapple, K. (1999). Good Practices in Knowledge Creation and Exchange. Focus Central, London.

Roknuzzaman, & Umemoto, K. (2013). Exploring LIS academics' responses to knowledge management. *Library Review, 62*(4/5), 293–311. https://doi.org/10.1108/LR-07-2012-0072

Rowley, J. (1999). What is knowledge management? *Library Management, 20*(8), 4.

Sarrafzadeh, M., Martin, B., & Hazeri, A. (2010). Knowledge management and its potential applicability for libraries. *Library Management, 31*(3), 198–212. https://doi.org/10.1108/01435121011027363

Senge, P. M. (2006). *The fifth discipline: The art and practice of the learning organization* (Rev. and updated). Doubleday/Currency.

Serrat, O. (2010). *Harvesting Knowledge.* ResearchGate. https://www.researchgate.net/publication/254582903_Harvesting_Knowledge

Skyrme, J. D. (1997). *Knowledge Management (David Skyrme Associates)*. Retrieved January 27, 2020, from http://www.skyrme.com/insights/22km.htm

Soto-Acosta, P., & Cegarra-Navarro, J.-G. (2016). New ICTs for Knowledge Management in Organizations. *Journal of Knowledge Management, 20*(3), 417–422. https://doi.org/10.1108/JKM-02-2016-0057

Thierauf, R. J. (1999). *Knowledge management systems for business*. Quorum Book.

Townley, C.T. (2001), Knowledge management and academic libraries. *College and Research Libraries*, Vol. 62 No. 1, . 44-55.

Tyndale, P. (2002). A taxonomy of Knowledge Management software tools: origins and applications. *Evaluation and Program Planning*, 25, 183-90.

Wai Tat, L., & Hase, S. (2007). Knowledge Management in the Malaysian Aerospace Industry. *Journal of Knowledge Management, 11*(1), 143–151. https://doi.org/10.1108/13673270710728295

Wiig, K. (1993), *Knowledge Management Foundations*, Schema Press, Arlington, TX

Wong, K.Y. and Aspinwall, E. (2004). Characterizing Knowledge Management in the small business environment. *Journal of Knowledge Management*, 8(3), 44-61.